A FIELD GUIDE TO

EVANGELICALS

and Their Habitat

A FIELD GUIDE TO

EVANGELICALS

and Their Habitat

JOEL KILPATRICK

HarperSanFrancisco
A Division of HarperCollinsPublishers

HarperCollins books may be purchased for educational, business, or sales promotional use. For information please write: Special Markets Department, HarperCollins Publishers, 10 East 53rd Street, New York, NY 10022.

HarperCollins Web site: http://www.harpercollins.com

HarperCollins®, 📖 ®, and HarperSanFrancisco™ are trademarks of HarperCollins Publishers

FIRST EDITION

Designed by Kris Tobiassen

Library of Congress Cataloging-in-Publication Data

Kilpatrick, Joel.
   A field guide to evangelicals and their habitat /Joel Kilpatrick.—1st ed.
      p. cm.

ISBN-10: 0–06–083696–2
ISBN-13: 978–0–06–083696–2

1. Religion—Humor. 2. Evangelicalism—Humor. I. Title.

PN6231.R4K55   2006
818'.607—dc22   2005050331

06 07 08 09 10 RRD(H) 10 9 8 7 6 5 4 3 2 1

CONTENTS

INTRODUCTION

Evangelical Christians in America now number 70 million people, and they are populating at an estimated rate of 3.2 children per family. They kicked electoral tail in the 2004 elections. And alarmingly oversized megachurches are sprouting up in suburbs from coast to coast—perhaps even near your favorite bar. For non-evangelicals, and for any civic-minded American, there has never been a greater need to understand this unique subculture. In fact, in our pluralistic society we *must* learn, in the words of a great American, to "all get along" so our cities don't devolve into something resembling Jerusalem, Darfur, or South Central L.A. We must put aside petty annoyances with each others' cultural habits and learn to tolerate, even enjoy, interacting with people of other religious faiths—no matter how abrasive we find them at first.

After all, evangelicals will not disappear from the American scene anytime soon—barring the Rapture. But we'll get to that later.

We at LarkNews have made it our mission to encourage cross-cultural understanding between evangelicals and other faith groups (see www.larknews.com). Now, for the first time, we have pooled our expertise and are offering this definitive guide to evangelicals and their way of life. Whether you come at the subject intrigued, confused, or even irritated, this first-of-its-kind field guide will help you discover evangelicals for yourself. In the forthcoming pages we will answer common questions, such as:

Do evangelicals really think everybody except them is going to hell?

Why are family values such a big deal to them?

How do evangelicals "have fun"?

At what point did they gain express control of the Republican Party?

Where do evangelicals reside, and why do they decorate their homes the way they do?

In a pinch, how do I talk like an evangelical?

This book is also for readers who may have more pressing concerns. Perhaps you are tired of your evangelical neighbor's weekly invitations to church and wish to know how to dampen his or her enthusiasm about your eternal soul.

Or maybe your niece just became engaged to an evangelical who will be coming to your house for Hanukkah. In these cases, and many more, you have picked up the right book!

Before we begin, let us offer a special note to those readers who have unusually high hostility levels toward evangelicals. Perhaps you were raised in a home where they were called "religious zealots," "right-wing fanatics," "narrow-minded bigots," "homeschooling Jesus freaks," or "Bible thumpers." It would be useful to assess your exact EHQ—Evangelical Hostility Quotient—so this book can offer specific help. Start by taking this brief test:

When you see someone toting a Bible in public, you:

1. **Think to yourself, "I wish that person would share his or her personal faith with me."**

2. **Feel grateful that our country ensures freedom of religion.**

3. **Express loud annoyance at this intrusive public display of faith.**

4. **Beat the person with available objects.**

The next time you see someone reading *Left Behind* on an airplane, you probably will:

1. **Ask to sit next to him or her and talk about spiritual things.**

2. **Politely pretend to sleep.**

3. **Request a different flight.**

4. **Find a way to dump the drink tray on him or her.**

A co-worker invites you to church. You:

1. **Accept.**

2. **Decline and begin prominently displaying your menorah, healing crystals, or Buddhist mandala.**

INTRODUCTION

3. Complain to a supervisor.

4. Create a special cup of coffee and copier toner for the co-worker.

Add up your responses, awarding one, two, three, or four points according to the number of each answer. Now compare results:

1–5—LOW EHQ: You are highly tolerant of evangelicals.

6–9—ELEVATED EHQ: You occasionally feel threatened or irritated by evangelicals.

10–12—DANGEROUSLY HIGH EHQ: Do *not* attempt to interact with an evangelical before reading this book!

No matter what your EHQ is, by the time you finish this guide you will be an "expert" in identifying and communicating with people who once frightened or puzzled you. We hope that within these pages you discover hours of pleasure in exploring this fascinating—and unavoidable—American way of life.

Happy sighting!

WHAT EVANGELICALS BELIEVE, PLUS A MASTER LIST OF WHO IS GOING TO HELL

Evangelicals believe in many things: the Father, Son, and Holy Spirit, church attendance, homeschooling, Fox News, abstinence, personal holiness, toupees, leisure suits, mission work, Dockers, golf, spanking, and dinner, early and often. But the natural starting point for identifying evangelicals by their beliefs is with their best-known doctrine: hell.

... IN A HANDBASKET

Evangelicals believe certain people are going to hell—you, for example, unless you already happen to be an evangelical. But behind the hellfire and brimstone talk are core beliefs that have deep meaning for evangelicals. Here are the three most important ones:

> **CORE BELIEF #1—Every person has an obligation to accept Jesus as his or her personal savior. The phrase "personal savior" is important, as it separates evangelicals from Catholic and Orthodox Christians who simply run their offspring through the gamut of religious rituals and call it square. To receive Christ "personally" means you have an epiphany about your personal sinfulness and Jesus's unique ability to rescue you from it. This is called "being saved." If you have not had this experience, you are considered "unsaved."**

> **CORE BELIEF #2—Jesus is coming back soon, probably tomorrow.**

> **CORE BELIEF #3—If you have neglected Core Belief #1, and Jesus does indeed come back tomorrow, you are going to hell.**

You may read as much evangelical theology as you like, but the essence is contained in these three beliefs. Clearly, these convictions give the evangelical worldview an amazing urgency. Through their lenses, every non-evangelical around them is dancing blindly on a plank overhanging the lake of fire. Evangelicals respond to this urgency with several reasonable behaviors:

They buy television airtime so televangelists can parade the latest in evangelical fashions and hairstyles before receptive American audiences.

They hit the streets and hand out frightening cartoon pamphlets, hoping these will lead people into lifelong, loving relationships with Jesus.

They confront people at work, in school hallways, and in plain view at other public sites about their "relationship with Christ."

They perform spiritual dramas to music, often in public squares, at school talent shows, and in other places where ridicule is guaranteed.

Each of these behaviors is designed, in its own fashion, to rescue people from hell. Perhaps this "fixation" with hell bothers you (readers with high EHQs take note). But from a sociological point of view, believing in hell is thought to be less violence-inducing than believing in heaven. Members of some religions go on suicide runs, thinking they will earn a vaunted position in heaven, including dozens of "extra virgins." In contrast, evangelicals don't want anyone* to die until they have received Jesus. There is no reward in evangelical theology for killing other people, and there hasn't been since about 1270 A.D. (The reward for enslaving people also ran out, in about 1865, and in some southern states in 1972.) For readers with an EHQ above 10, this may be the first attractive thing they have ever learned about evangelicals.

Except, perhaps, death row inmates, abortionists, truculent Arabs, Democrats, homosexuals, and ACLU members.

Chapter 1
WHAT EVANGELICALS
BELIEVE, PLUS A
MASTER LIST OF WHO
IS GOING TO HELL

To be extra clear, let's chart it out:

	Going to HEAVEN!	Going to HELL	Will Be Locked in a Room with Richard Simmons and Charo in HELL
Evangelicals	✔		
ACLU members		✔	
Al Franken		✔	
Barbra Streisand		✔	
Buddhists		✔	
Catholics		✔	
The Clintons		✔	
Dalai Lama		✔	
Dan Rather		✔	
Divorce lawyers		✔	
The French			✔
Hollywood types		✔	
Homosexuals		✔	
Jews		✔	
Jews for Jesus	✔		
Michael Moore		✔	
Mel Gibson	✔		
Mormons		✔	
Muslims		✔	
The *New York Times* (the whole staff)		✔	
O. J. Simpson		✔	
The Osbournes		✔	
The Pope		✔	
Ronald Reagan	✔		
Ron Reagan Jr.		✔	
Ted Turner		✔	
SpongeBob SquarePants		✔	

BANDS THAT WILL BE PLAYING IN HELL

AC/DC—Guitarist Angus Young won kudos from the evangelical community for dressing in a smart black blazer, but upon releasing "Highway to Hell" and other unmentionable tunes, the band assured itself a spot on the Hades main stage.

KISS—The band better known among evangelicals as Knights In Satan's Service is said to have stomped baby chicks to death during live performances, not to mention the tacky demonic getup that made them look like possessed members of the cast of *Cats*. Evangelicals firmly believe that provocateur Gene Simmons and pals will rock on forever in the lake of fire.

BLACK SABBATH—The band's very name, plus the decision to put angels smoking cigarettes on an album cover, make Black Sabbath hell's favorite band already. There are hopes for a reunion with Ozzy once all members arrive.

LED ZEPPELIN—Plant, Page, and crew will play "Stairway to Heaven" backwards for eternity, an acknowledgment that the song was indeed rife with satanically inspired messages recorded backwards and intended to have a subliminal effect on teenage listeners.

MARILYN MANSON—Rumor has it that even Satan is afraid of the ghoulish performer, who may be shunted into a less populated region of hell because he poses a takeover threat.

ARTISTS WHO WILL BE PLAYING IN HEAVEN

MICHAEL W. SMITH—Imagine a billion redeemed souls singing "Friends Are Friends Forever" with Christian music's boy wonder on the piano. It's enough to give any evangelical chills.

THE GAITHERS' FINAL HOMECOMING—Two straight eons of nonstop nostalgia.

PAT BOONE—Though he nearly lost favorite-son status in 1999 with his foray into heavy metal music, Boone remains the top performer on heaven's bill. He will croon from center stage, in his standard white bucks.

DEBBY BOONE—Yes, that song . . . forever.

PURGATORY AND THE POPE

Purgatory is an entirely Catholic creation and is completely foreign to evangelicals, who prefer their beliefs in sharp black and white. Why, they wonder, would God create purgatory when heaven and hell do the job of separation so well? The concept of purgatory is what some evangelicals, in their darker moments, expect from the religion that gave the world Mary worship and the Kennedys.

As for the Pope, evangelicals don't recognize him, and there is no Pope-like leader within the evangelical world. The closest thing they have is Billy Graham, but he makes no doctrine. He is only an itinerant preacher who gained renown and became a close spiritual adviser to half a dozen lying, cheating U.S. presidents.

To most evangelicals, the Pope is nothing more than an object of curiosity—and the punch line of some terrific jokes. Some see him as a decent man stuck in an apostate religion. Others—those who chart out end-times events in their spare time and memorize the Book of Revelation— see him as an abomination, even the anti-Christ. But because he shares many evangelical political positions (the death penalty excepted), there is a sense that he is within the family. Many evangelicals look at the Pope and think, "If he weren't the Pope, but instead a plumber from Cincinnati, I bet he would vote Republican straight down the ticket. And that's all right with me." For this reason, most evangelicals don't mind the Pope. After all, he makes Democratic presidential candidates squirm every four years by bringing up their abortion stance, and any religious leader who does that can't be all bad.

THE RAPTURE

Here is another major evangelical belief. For evangelicals, the Rapture promises to be the world's biggest I Told You So, providing final vindication for the unusual way they lived on this planet. They expect to disappear one day in the blink of an eye, journeying through the air to their home in heaven, where they will peer over and watch *Left Behind: The Reality Series* play out on Earth. This promises to deliver hours of enjoyment for leisure-minded evangelicals in their heavenly mansions.

Rapture Safety cards prepare parishioners, airline-style

PINE BLUFF, Ark. — Last Days Bible Church has taken a novel step to prepare people for the Rapture: under each seat in the sanctuary is an airline-style safety card giving instructions for what to do when the Rapture takes place.

"When the Rapture happens we want saved and unsaved people alike to get through the experience safely," says Eckers. "We're especially concerned that no one get trampled, because, of course, the ushers will be gone."

Chapter 1
WHAT EVANGELICALS
BELIEVE, PLUS A
MASTER LIST OF WHO
IS GOING TO HELL

The only evangelicals who don't look forward to the Rapture are teenage boys, who desperately want to have sex before the Rapture occurs. Teen evangelical boys usually drift to sleep each night praying fervently that God will delay the Rapture until they can lose their virginity. The threat of Rapture also helps to explain the young age at which evangelicals get married and begin breeding.

But even evangelicals don't claim to have all the answers about the Rapture. For example, will people's clothes be left behind when they are caught away (which brings to mind the tricky theological matter of naked evangelicals suspended in midair)? And what will happen to airplanes and heavy machinery when "Raptured" operators disappear? Millions of unsaved people might be put in positions of peril, which is why evangelicals prudently steer their children away from careers, such as commercial piloting, ferry operating, and long-haul trucking, in which their sudden absence will jeopardize the lives of others. Besides, those occupations tend to encourage on-the-job drunkenness and sex with one's co-workers or one's self, all of which lies outside the evangelical scheme of good habits.

Some evangelicals debate the proper pose to strike when the Rapture occurs. Some prefer the "Superman" pose, one knee slightly bent, arms held heavenward with one higher than the other. Others prefer to practice a flange shape, like a badminton shuttlecock, which is more effective if one's body must penetrate ceilings, tree branches, car roofs, etc. It is unknown if there will be any warning that the Rapture is about to occur—perhaps a single note on the angelical trumpet before the saints are airborne. It is known that there will not be enough time for unsaved people to change their minds, hence they will be "left behind" and the Tim LaHaye–Jerry Jenkins series will slip quietly from the "fiction" to the "nonfiction" category on the *New York Times* best-seller list.

The Bible says nobody knows when the Rapture will take place, but God has been known, in his more jocular moments, to reveal the time and date of the Rapture to

---

HELPFUL HEADLINE

RAPTURE JOKE PROVOKES HEART ATTACK

AUSTIN, TEX.—Herbert Washington, whom co-workers at Significant Plastics Inc. say was unduly concerned with the Rapture and the second coming of Christ, suffered a serious heart attack when co-workers pretended they'd been caught away without him.

Last Tuesday they lay work outfits on their chairs and hid in a supply room, and when Herbert came back from the restroom, he thought the Rapture had occurred. The janitor, an outspoken Muslim, pretended to have witnessed everyone disappear and ran around the office feigning panic. Herbert fell to the ground clutching his heart and screaming, "I knew you'd forget me, Jesus! What did I do wrong?" He was taken to a local hospital. The employees emerged, sobered, from the supply room and gathered up their extra clothes.

"We didn't mean to scare him to death," says one woman. "He's just always talking about it, so today we decided to turn the tables on him."

Washington underwent bypass surgery and is recovering well and "digging into the Bible like never before," says his wife.

From LarkNews.com, a good source of Christian news

certain servants of his, then change his mind and postpone it, leaving entire congregations on mountaintops or in remote rural locations looking very silly indeed. This is evidence of God's sense of humor and should not be chalked up to the sheer stupidity or hubris of the people involved. If you see them slinking back to town, pat them on the back and say, "Maybe next time." Then consider how close they must be to God to have him play a practical joke like that on them.

HEAVEN

To evangelicals, heaven is the ultimate gated community. According to the Book of Revelation, there will be no criminals, welfare recipients, sexual deviants, "unbelieving" people, or "cowards" in heaven. This is the same irresistible portrait of bliss evangelicals see in Republican campaign literature, which promises a land "just over yonder" where bad people are expelled and all the good people dress modestly (in body-length white robes) and are unbelievably rich.

FINDING GOD'S WILL

Evangelicals spend much time and energy trying to find what they call "God's will." God's will is defined as something that God wants very much for your life but that he refuses to share with you directly. Evangelicals believe it is their job to figure out what he is thinking through prayer, fasting, Bible reading, and watching *The O'Reilly Factor*.

Finding God's will is like living with a mute and uncooperative spouse who won't reveal what he or she

Some evangelicals believe it is impossible to lose your salvation at all. You might accept Jesus as a four-year-old, live like Hugh Hefner, and still make the Pearly Gates.

wants and who is becoming more anxious, angry, and sad by the moment. It can take years to fully ascertain God's will for one's life, and even after it has been discovered, one must still carry it out with a level of uncertainty and a persistent suspicion that one is doing one's own will instead of God's will. In evangelical circles, one is not allowed to have a will. If one discovers that one's will still exists, one must ask God in treacly worship songs for one's will to be overcome and obliterated. Any evangelical found in possession of a will is thought to be in danger of hell (see the following section, "Backsliding").

God's will also provides a convenient "out" for those evangelicals who wish to do nothing. If you are inclined to chug along in life without accomplishing anything in particular, the proper wording to establish your cover is "I'm waiting on God, seeking his will in my life. I just want to be sure what it is." One may go on indefinitely in this condition, accomplishing nothing, living with one's parents, with the full respect of one's evangelical friends.

BACKSLIDING

One of the most grievous states of existence, in the evangelical mind, is to be backslidden. To backslide means to walk away from a former confession of faith in Christ. Nobody knows exactly how far into perdition you must slip to be considered backslidden. Indeed, some evangelicals believe it is impossible to lose your salvation at all. You might accept Jesus as a four-year-old, live like Hugh Hefner, and still make the Pearly Gates.

Others, in contrast, believe that salvation is lost and regained many times in a single day—for lying to your

MAN, 91, DIES WAITING FOR WILL OF GOD

TUPELO, MISS.—Walter Houston, described by family members as a devoted Christian, died Monday after waiting seventy years for God to give him clear direction about what to do with his life.

"He hung around the house and prayed a lot, but just never got that confirmation," his wife Ruby says. "Sometimes he thought he heard God's voice, but then he wouldn't be sure, and he'd start the process all over again."

Houston, she says, never really figured out what his life was about, but felt content to pray continuously about what he might do for the Lord. Whenever he was about to take action, he would pull back, "because he didn't want to disappoint God or go against him in any way," Ruby says. "He was very sensitive to always remaining in God's will. That was primary to him."

Friends say they liked Walter, though he seemed not to capitalize on his talents.

"Walter had a number of skills he never got around to using," says longtime friend Timothy Burns. "He worked very well with wood and had a storyteller side to him too. I always told him, 'Take a risk. Try something new if you're not happy,' but he was too afraid of letting the Lord down."

To his credit, they say, Houston, who worked mostly as a handyman, was able to pay off the mortgage on the couple's modest home.

From LarkNews.com, a good source of Christian news

mother or even wondering about the breeding habits of hamsters. You might live like Mother Teresa, then have a single stray thought while crossing the street ("I wonder what Julia Roberts's breasts feel like?"), get struck by a car, and find yourself singing in the devil's bass section.

In general, most evangelicals agree that the following are examples of backslidden conditions and behaviors:

Lives with girlfriend or boyfriend

Is a fan of original HBO programming

Drinks alcohol (except on West Coast)

Smokes occasional cigar or pipe (except in Australia or England or at meetings of the C. S. Lewis Society)

Uses foul language (except for shock-evangelist Tony Campolo)

Consorts with Unitarians (no exceptions)

The way to get out of one's backslidden condition is commonly agreed on: you must "repent and ask Jesus for forgiveness." Evangelicals believe Jesus does not offer forgiveness unless you ask for it directly. He is a stickler about this. You must also "repent," which, of course, means to "pent" again.

Keep in mind that you cannot be backslidden unless you have first been saved. If you have never been saved, in evangelical parlance, you are not "backslidden," you are "lost."

Having covered the basics of evangelical beliefs, it's time to begin identifying real-life evangelicals in the world around you—certainly a frightening proposition for some readers. In the next chapter, we will discuss evangelical habitats, special markings, and the rich variety of vocalizations they use to identify one another and telegraph spiritual messages to the unsaved people around them.

And if your purpose in reading this book is to learn how to avoid evangelicals, we'll give you a crib sheet on that too.

IDENTIFYING EVANGELICALS IN THE FIELD

It's not always easy to tell evangelicals from other over-weight white Americans. They don't wear yarmulkes or put red dots on their foreheads like followers of other religions, and they don't always wear their Republican Party lapel buttons. For those who wish to observe and study evangelicals, this poses a strategic challenge.

But just as a bird-watcher stands quietly in a forest and trains himself to hear and see the various birds there, so you can tune your senses to perceive previously unno-ticed cues that whisper—or in some cases shout—that you are in the presence of an evangelical.

By learning to spot evangelicals before they spot you, you can also avoid the Personal Testimony Zone—

that place where evangelicals relate their "salvation experience" and try to convince you of your need for a personal relationship with Jesus. Unless you find the PTZ particularly stimulating or amusing—and unless you have several free hours to spend on the subject and don't mind getting follow-up calls from an outreach pastor who has been alerted to your spiritual curiosity—you should maintain a low profile and observe evangelicals on the sly.

Thankfully, evangelicals have distinct habits and habitats that set them apart as a breed. This chapter offers tips, tactics, and tools to help you spy out evangelicals wherever you go. Soon you will be able to impress your friends by correctly identifying evangelicals at fifty paces in a crowded mall with nothing more than a glance.

EVANGELICAL HANGOUTS

Where can evangelicals be sighted and observed? To the chagrin of some readers, the answer is: virtually anywhere. Venture to any region in America (except New York's Upper West Side) and evangelicals will have already moved in and established a neighborhood Bible study.

But wherever they go, evangelicals stick to predictable habitats—habitats designed, in most cases, to maintain their personal holiness or to save them money. The most popular habitats are as follows.

Wal-Mart

A bastion of midwestern sensibility, Wal-Mart has shrewdly positioned itself as an extension of the evangelical home, offering a sacred place for evangelicals to buy cereal, kneesocks, and My First Semiautomatic Rifle.

Wal-Mart earns kudos from evangelicals by:

a) Placing surrogate grandparent greeters at the door, subtly reaffirming traditional family values.

b) Paying employees and underage Chinese factory workers less-than-living wages, which appeals strongly to the evangelical sense of thrift.

c) Bowdlerizing the CD racks and playing wholesome music over the in-store sound system—no foul rap songs or pulsing rock beats, as you might hear at the fashion boutique.

d) Purging the readers' aisle of *Maxim* magazine and subversive George Carlin books that might taint little eyes.

In tacit partnership, Wal-Mart and its "silent shopping majority" have created the marketplace equivalent of a mega-church. No wonder Wal-Mart now accounts for 8 percent of U.S. consumer purchases—which is almost a tithe.

Evangelistic Crusades

Though they consider themselves already to be "saved," evangelicals still love attending evangelistic events—a kind of spiritual spawning. Preteen evangelical girls rush the stage, screaming and fainting as their favorite "celebrity" evangelist preaches. Older saints' hearts are warmed by the familiar cadence of a well-crafted sermon.

Christians plan to be offended by next Eminem album

DETROIT — Rapper Eminem is taking a year off, but Christians are already preparing to be offended by his next album.

"I'm good and ready to be outraged," says Earl Gillani, 46, who has been practicing his shocked expression and the "don't you bring that garbage into this house" speech he plans to give his teenager.

Mother Maureen Dafney cringes at the very thought of Eminem's next musical offering.

"It pains me to think of it," she says. "I'm primed for disappointment."

Some parents simply want the relief of knowing what they have waited to be offended by.

Many other evangelicals find that, having given up clubbing and drinking, and with the general scarcity of bowling alleys these days, they have nothing better to do on Friday nights—especially if the prayer meeting has been moved to Tuesdays. For this reason, 98.7 percent of the audience at any given evangelistic event is already saved.

Evangelical-Owned Businesses

Evangelicals are keen to patronize businesses owned by fellow believers, and every city has dozens of such "undercover" evangelical enterprises. It may never have occurred to you that when you shopped for a loan at Trinity Mortgage, called Cornerstone Septic Repair, or wandered into the Solid Rock Tile Shop, you were inadvertently supporting an evangelical-owned business. Readers with high EHQs may take a moment to stop hyperventilating before reading on.

Some evangelical businesses stencil an IXOYE fish or scripture verse on the window, alerting you to the owner's spiritual affiliation. But many simply choose a name that brings to mind some aspect of the gospel. This mental coaxing serves as a potential "witness" to non-evangelicals, who may subconsciously be inspired to reconsider the claims of Christ. It also telegraphs to evangelicals that any dollars spent there go directly into the Kingdom.

Here are the types of names that indicate evangelical ownership:

White Dove Nail Salon
Paradise Bait and Tackle
Last Days Auto Repair

> Fully half of all evangelical injuries are incurred while fighting over the last tongful of bacon at all-you-can-eat buffets.

If you have a free afternoon, hang around a business you suspect to be run by evangelicals. Sooner or later a customer will come in and be greeted with a hug and a "How are you, brother?" That's all the confirmation you need.

Denny's Restaurant, Sundays, 11:00 A.M.–2:00 P.M.

In a ritual as time-honored as church itself, evangelicals stampede to low-priced sit-down restaurants immediately after Sunday services to celebrate their salvation with fellowship, flapjacks, and enough biscuits and gravy to shock even Paul Prudhomme. Fully half of all evangelical injuries are incurred while fighting over the last tongful of bacon at all-you-can-eat buffets.

Why do evangelicals aim so low on the culinary totem pole? Because Sunday brunch is a humble adjunct to the sermon, not a high point in itself. The exotic foods at fine-'n'-fancy restaurants militate against the simplicity and straightforwardness of the gospel. (The Bible calls the gospel "milk" and "meat," never "escargot on a bed of fennel and spinach.") There is no good reason, evangelicals believe, to put so much thought and creativity into food preparation, and it probably means the chef is either gay or, worse, French.

And really, given a choice between salmon canapés and piles of link sausage at the all-day-breakfast buffet, which would you choose?

If you are able to rouse yourself on Sunday morning after that night of decidedly non-evangelical carousing, head to a herd-'em-in place. (Any restaurant with a name ending in a "y" sound should do.) Perch at the lunch

Chapter 2
IDENTIFYING
EVANGELICALS IN
THE FIELD

EVANGELICAL VACATION SPOTS

BRANSON, MISSOURI

Branson sits in a geographical sweet spot, about as far as you can get from both Los Angeles (1,653 miles) and New York City (1,205 miles) without being in Oklahoma. That distance from "places that matter" suits evangelicals just fine. Like a little slice of heaven, the city of Branson envelops them in old-time values at every turn. Attend a gospel sing before brunch, an Andy Williams show at night, and Christian-owned and -operated amusement parks in between. Then head up to Springfield (30 miles away) and tour the headquarters of the Assemblies of God, the largest and most overlooked Christian denomination in the world.

> WARNING: The riskiest time to be on Branson's roads is between 4:00 and 6:00 P.M., when elderly tour bus groups fight one another to get into the early-bird specials. To avoid injury, stay in your hotel and watch VeggieTales or *The Omega Code*. That's all that will be available on Pay-Per-View.

Also, if you happen to find yourself in the firearms section of a Wal-Mart in Branson, you are in the very eye of the evangelical universe. Pause, reflect—then run.

COLORADO SPRINGS, COLORADO

Home of dozens of major evangelical ministries, Colorado Springs is the closest thing evangelicals have to a Mecca, though Orlando and Dallas, which also offer cheap land, are becoming popular as well.

Of particular note is Focus on the Family headquarters, founded by Dr. James Dobson, whose book *Dare to Discipline* established spanking as a competitive sport among evangelicals. (Benjamin "Mr. Permissive"

Spock had a few cute theories but knew nothing about handling five children under the age of eight.) From all over the United States, evangelicals take vacation time to come to the eighty-one-acre Focus on the Family campus and pay homage to Dobson, their patron saint of parenting.

counter and observe how the atmosphere shifts from sedate senior citizens enjoying their 10 percent discounts to jocular evangelicals who bring with them a jubilance at having just worshiped together and a sincere enthusiasm for fried food.

Listen to their conversations; hear the kids tell Mom and Dad what they learned at Sunday school. Hear Mom complain mildly about the new worship leader. Hear Dad pat his belly and say he is looking forward to his Sunday nap. Then watch as Dad tips the waitress 5 percent and encourages the kids to top off their tummies with one more trip to the buffet.

WHERE EVANGELICALS FEAR TO TREAD

There are specific places evangelicals will not go. Readers who want to avoid evangelicals may go a lifetime without encountering them by sticking to the following establishments.

Bars, Nightclubs, and Pool Halls

You will not find evangelicals in places that encourage drunkenness, fornication, dancing, or fighting with pool

cues. The *only* time they might duck into such a place is to hang a poster for a Christian concert or a notice about an alcohol recovery program at their church. Evangelicals don't want to make the mistake Jesus made in hanging around society's lowlifes and becoming known as wine-bibbers and drunkards—a reputation that put a major crimp in his earthly ministry.

R-Rated Movies

There are plenty of reasons for evangelicals to skip the theater, from the crass depiction of women's bare bosoms and tender parts to the compulsive use of the Lord's name as a curse word. Depictions of depraved violence are verboten too—except for *The Passion of the Christ,* which became a mega-hit because of repeat viewings by evangelical families.

If you care to spend an entertaining, evangelical-free evening, select an R-rated movie, preferably one that promises plenty of sex and violence, and afterward cap it off with a drink at the Bump & Grind.

Liquor Stores

Though there are plenty of useful non-alcoholic items at liquor stores, evangelicals would sooner step into Hades for a pack of gum. Not only is it terrifying for them to be in a place stacked to the ceiling with the devil's drink and displaying racks of girlie magazines by the door, but if a brother or sister in the Lord saw them walk out of a liquor store, their place on the Usher Team might suddenly come into question.

Also, most liquor stores are operated by Arabs, Indians, or men in turbans, and evangelicals prefer not to give their

> Though there are plenty of useful non-alcoholic items at liquor stores, evangeli- cals would sooner step into Hades for a pack of gum.

TYPICAL EVANGELICAL ERRAND LIST

WAL-MART—lightbulbs, pantyhose, bullets for the Winchester

HOLY GROUNDS CAFÉ—low-fat manna-nut muffin, half pound of Philip's Ethiopian coffee beans

CROSSWAY ELECTRICAL—fix big-screen TV for neighborhood showings of Jesus film

BOX OFFICE—tickets for the baseball game (no-beer section)

CHICK-FIL-A—lunch (use coupon from church bulletin)

THE CHURCH—retrieve sweater from lost and found, drop off tithe check

BIBLE BOOKSTORE—Beginner's Study Bible for new neighbors, in case opportunity arises

WAL-MART AGAIN—because it feels good

hard-earned money to people of other religions if they can help it.

New Age Stores

Just walking by these goddess-inspired spiritual nooks gives evangelicals the creeps—like they have strayed into a dark corner of a Frank Peretti novel. In spite of the lure of terrific

instrumental music and decorative candles, evangelicals boycott New Age stores and stick instead with worshipfully Yanni-esque John Tesh albums and cozy Thomas Kinkade candles by Glade.

If you have been forced to be in the presence of evangelicals and you need to detox, duck into the local Age of Aquarius store and breathe easy. It is an Evangelical-Free Zone.

IDENTIFYING EVANGELICALS ON THE ROADWAYS

If you still fear the possibility of face-to-face contact with evangelicals, you may observe them from your automobile—a private "blind on wheels."

Though evangelicals don't prefer one make or model of vehicle, keep an eye out for sensible cars—Toyotas and Hondas with multiple child seats in the back and Econoline passenger vans to ferry the neighborhood kids to and from vacation Bible school. *Note:* You won't see evangelicals driving high-end Mercedes or Italian cars unless they are the leader of a major television ministry.

Cruise by public parks, which during the day attract high percentages of evangelicals. After going batty teaching five homeschooled children about the faith of the founding fathers, evangelical moms decamp there so the kids can run off their energy before it manifests itself as sin. Look for frazzled women reading *The Purpose-Driven Life* while their kids take over the jungle gym.

But the easiest way to spot evangelicals from your automobile is to examine the rear bumpers of cars around you. Like everything else in life, evangelicals believe their car bumper's ultimate purpose is to provoke Jesus-related thoughts in people's minds. To that end, they bedeck their cars' backsides with a delightful diversity of Christian sentiments, from the patriotically belligerent:

AMERICA, BLESS GOD!

To the whimsical:

DON'T DRIVE FASTER THAN YOUR ANGELS CAN FLY

To the corrective:

GOD'S LAST NAME IS NOT DAMN

To the comedically off-beat:

IN CASE OF RAPTURE, THIS CAR WILL BE UNMANNED!

For evangelicals, an undecorated bumper is a sin for which God will hold them accountable the moment they walk into heaven. A car is not just a car—it's prime advertising space, given by God for the conversion of other drivers as one drives hither and thither all over town. Perhaps while a needy nonbeliever is idling at a red light in a moment of personal crisis, he or she will view the "No God, no peace. KNOW God, KNOW peace" bumper sticker and experience a Pauline epiphany. Perhaps that "Life is fragile, handle with prayer" sticker you see on the car ahead of you in the drive-through will provide a final spiritual nudge, leading you to pull into your garage, weep, and surrender your life to Christ.

The time-honored IXOYE fish is another stalwart of the evangelical bumper. IXOYE is the Greek word *icthus*, which means "fish," and the letters stand for the first letters

IXOYE war spreads to Wisconsin

RACINE — Hostilities between motorists brandishing 'IXOYE' fish and 'Darwin' fish broke into open conflict after years of simmering anger.

"This thing finally boiled over here," said a police officer at a Target store parking lot where skirmishes had broken out. Six cars were damaged and the ground was littered with silver shards of plastic, the remains of so-called "message fish."

"It was pretty vicious," said Bill Henley, who witnessed the attack by 'IXOYE' guerillas. "They threw rocks at the windows of any ca...

of "Jesus Christ, Son of God, Savior." Most evangelicals don't know this, but they do know that the subtle silver emblem offers membership in a secret club of believers, recalling the early days of the faith when Christians sneaked around the Roman empire building *ecclesia maxime* and avoiding nutty caesars.

These days the IXOYE fish serves a practical purpose of telling fellow evangelicals, "Don't honk at me! We'll be spending eternity together." But a secularist backlash has spawned an assortment of clever "Darwin" fish-with-feet—causing deep woundedness among evangelicals. They have learned to cope with prayerless public schools and gays on prime-time television. But to have godless motorists make sport of their sacred symbol? It's almost too much for them to handle.

Evangelicals have responded to Darwin fish as Jesus would have—by depicting IXOYE fish violently eating the Darwin fish and showing the Darwin fish upside down and dead. Some evangelicals wish there were a universally recognized "evolutionist" or "secularist" symbol they could desecrate in return, but there isn't, so their efforts at retaliation are somewhat limited.

ALL IS VANITY

As you drive around town spotting evangelicals here and there, be sure to also check the license plate itself, which is the surest indicator. That LV4JSUS you see is not a random assignment of letters and numbers; rather, it's another attempt to convey a gospel message to you. Here are a few examples of what you might see on an evangelical vanity plate:

GD ISGR8

IM SVED

GSPL CAR

GOT JSUS

Evangelicals especially love to put abbreviated Bible verses on their plates. These can be decoded like so:

JHN 316 John 3:16: "For God so loved the world that he gave his one and only Son, that whoever believes in him shall not perish but have eternal life."

MAT 74 Matthew 7:4: "Ask and it will be given to you; seek and you will find; knock and the door will be opened to you."

ROM 828 Romans 8:28: "And we know that in all things God works for the good of those who love him, who have been called according to his purpose."

With these suggestions, evangelicals hope to steer you to the neglected Bible you've been keeping in your glove compartment.

Vanity plates that convey Bible verses are so popular that nearly every passage in the Bible has been snatched up by eager evangelical motorists. A DMV check reveals that only a few Bible-themed plates remain available in most states. They are:

SLMN 45 Song of Solomon 4:5: "Your breasts are perfect; they are twin deer feeding among lilies."

EZK 1635 Ezekiel 16:35: "Therefore, you prostitute, listen to this message from the Lord!"

JDG 317 Judges 3:17: "He brought the tax money to Eglon, who was very fat."

Interestingly, mischievous secular drivers have not tried to tweak evangelical motorists with plates that say things like:

SATAN 1

DEVL CAR

HLZ AWSM

Perhaps they know that, given such extreme provocation, evangelicals aren't beyond putting a rock through their windshield.

If the bumper sticker says . . .	The driver is probably . . .
"My six children are honor students in our Homeschool Program"	An evangelical
"My kid can beat the hell out of your honor student"	A non-evangelical driving an El Camino
"Jesus on board"	An evangelical
"Pro-Child, Pro-Choice"	A non-evangelical gold-level member of the local NPR station
"Honk if you love Jesus!"	An evangelical
"Imagine whirled peas"	Still in counseling about the 2000 and 2004 elections
"Pat Robertson 2008"	An evangelical
"Christians make me suuue happy"	Alan Dershowitz

LICENSE PLATE MISTAKE A HEADACHE FOR CHRISTIAN MOTORIST

SAN LUIS OBISPO, CALIF.—Sally Warner, 43, became a Christian while reading the biblical book of Titus. A week later she submitted a form to the DMV requesting a personalized license plate. But her request for a plate reading "TITUS 4U" arrived at her home reading "TITS 4U."

"I was crushed," Warner says. "I couldn't bring myself to put them on my car. The DMV people have been very sympathetic, but they insist I use these plates until new ones arrive."

Warner, a nurse, owns one car and has to drive to work every day. Now other motorists honk at her on the highway, and men make rude "breast-squeezing" gestures, she says, "and not just truckers." She often finds notes with phone numbers left on her windshield.

"All I can think is, 'This is what I get for trying to share the best thing that ever happened to me?'" Warner tells a reporter through tears.

The DMV says they are expediting Warner's request, and that there may be an upside to the unfortunate episode.

"Her plate may actually be a collector's item," says a DMV spokeswoman. "We're not allowed to put certain words on license plates and 'tits' is certainly one of them. We're puzzled how this happened."

From LarkNews.com, a good source of Christian news

HOW TO TELL IN A SINGLE LUNCH HOUR IF YOUR CO-WORKER IS AN EVANGELICAL

Not all evangelicals are "live-it-out-loud" types who badger people to attend church. In fact, most evangelicals live quietly and don't attract attention. Your own workplace is probably full of evangelicals whom you have not yet identified. But perhaps a relentlessly cheery and outgoing co-worker has you and other employees wondering, "Is this person a passionate evangelical trying to make a good impression, or is he or she merely friendly in a Gary, Indiana, sort of way?" Keep in mind that friendly people are not necessarily evangelical. In fact, according to evangelical theology, many friendly people will end up in hell, alongside a lot of really terrible people who earned their way in.

The solution: go to lunch with your suspected evangelical co-worker and put him through a series of moral challenges. Within the hour, the answer should be clear.

Start off quietly. If at all possible, allow him to drive so that you can look for Christian bumper stickers on his vehicle. In his car, take note of the radio station that pops on immediately after the car is started. If the music has an unusually positive message, and if the only advertiser seems to be the local crisis pregnancy center, it is almost certainly a Christian radio station. If the radio is off, and you are feeling bold, ask if you can rifle through the tapes and CDs floating around under the seat. If you have never heard of the artists, and if the song titles include words like "glorify" and "praise," you are probably riding with an evangelical. On the other hand, his mother may be trying to convert him by sneaking Christian tapes into his car, so don't jump to conclusions. Also check the rearview mirror for a "Smile! God loves you" pin, or the classic "Please be patient. God isn't finished with me yet."

Note which route your co-worker takes to the restaurant. Does he go out of his way to avoid driving through "seedy" sections of town where the porn shops and "men's clubs" are? If so, either he is an evangelical or he has an outstanding bill at one of these establishments. (If your co-worker suddenly raises a hand toward a business and says, "I pray that den of filth would *shut down*. I say be *cursed* in the name of Jesus," you are out to lunch not only with an evangelical, but with a charismatic evangelical, a special type that some would say is already out to lunch.)

See if you can convince him to take you to Hooters. If he refuses, suggest a local bar and grill, or at the very least a Chinese restaurant where you know plenty of carved Buddhas and Asian gods are displayed. Does the atmosphere in any of these places make him uncomfortable? Does he shrink into himself, averting his eyes from the flashing beer signs, busty waitstaff, or leering idols?

For conversation, introduce minor irritants to see how he reacts. Mention how "lucky" he is to have that new corner office. Evangelicals cannot stomach the idea of luck and chance. With God, they will tell you, nothing happens by chance, and so he will probably correct you by saying, "I really am blessed." If you feel particularly pert, press the point by saying, "Fortune is really smiling on you, and the Hand of Fate is clearly at work in your life. You should consider yourself lucky." Your co-worker might grind his teeth and—readers with high EHQs, beware—lose all tact and declare his fealty to Christ loudly enough

Family boycotts everything

JOPLIN, Mo. — Three years ago, the Molina family took a moral stand: they would not patronize any company which had connections to abortions, homosexual rights, pornography or other objectionable causes.

This month, that decision reached its zenith as the Molinas' boycott now covers every product on the U.S. market.

"Our lives have narrowed down to a few select products," says mother Carly, peeling homegrown carrots. The children play with splintery wooden toys hewn from a nearby tree. For entertainment they watch old Lassie movies on a VCR ma[?] by an obscure Korean compan[?]

Chapter 2
IDENTIFYING
EVANGELICALS IN
THE FIELD

to attract the attention of other diners. This would be unpleasant, but at least you would have succeeded in figuring out his evangelical status. Order a beer and take the rest of the lunch hour easy.

When the food comes, does he lapse into a quick moment of silence before taking the first bite? Most evangelicals feel deeply ingrained guilt if they begin a meal without praying. See if you can keep him talking before he digs in. Note his level of frustration as you disallow any pause in the conversation so he cannot say grace.

If that doesn't work, regale him with stories of what you did on a recent Sunday morning, focusing on some consumption-oriented hobby like jet-skiing. This will rankle your colleague, for whom Sunday mornings mean church, only church, and nothing but church. Look for signs of agitation as you describe how much fun you had during your time of godless recreation. You might also throw in a couple of curse words and watch for a wince.

Mention that the boss is going to make everyone stay late on Wednesdays until the project is done. Does he blanch? Wednesday evening is likely to be the time for his midweek church service.

If you are at a Chinese restaurant, make a big deal of the fortune in your fortune cookie after the meal. Insist that your co-worker read his fortune aloud, then verbally contemplate what it might mean for his future. If a newspaper is handy, read his horoscope to him.

If you somehow managed to drag your male co-worker to Hooters, suggest leaving a 25 percent tip for your waitress and "her beautiful assistants." Then offer to send the uneaten portion of the appetizer home with your co-worker

READER WORKSHEET

Do you suspect some of your co-workers are evangelicals? Perhaps it would be helpful to detail your suspicions on this worksheet.

SAMPLE LIST

Co-worker Name	Job	Reason for Suspicion
Timothy	Assistant manager	Doesn't attend company parties at the Keg & Cleaver
Susan	Cafeteria server	Says, "Blessings to you" and wears a cross necklace
Doug	Maintenance guy	Cell phone ring plays "Amazing Grace"

YOUR CO-WORKERS

_____

_____

_____

_____

_____

_____

_____

_____

_____

_____

in a clearly marked Hooters take-home bag so his wife doesn't have to cook dinner.

On the way back to work, ask if he would mind stopping at the liquor store so you can pick up some lip balm. Invite him into the store with you. Does this make him nervous? Does he slink down in his seat to avoid being seen, in case his pastor drives by?

If after this rigorous going-over you still haven't figured out if your co-worker is evangelical, either he has earned your respect by being highly skilled at hiding his affiliation or he is just an everyday Joe. But there are a few more tricks to discover his spiritual leanings.

EVANGELICAL ACCOUTREMENTS

While evangelicals single-handedly keep the midpriced clothing industry alive, they also heed the fashion world's number one rule: accessorize, accessorize, accessorize. In fact, apart from their accessories—WWJD bracelets, cross necklaces, and that splash of "Left Behind: The Fragrance"—evangelicals can be difficult to spot.

In the wild, birds, frogs, and other animals broadcast certain messages with their plumage and skin coloring. Fancy feathers say, "I'm looking for a mate." Red stripes say, "I'm poisonous." For evangelicals, every fashion choice says, "I know Jesus, and you should too." They broadcast this on key chains, necklaces, office decorations, screen savers, T-shirts, and, in some parts of Texas, belt buckles.

If you are puzzling about someone's evangelical status, keep a sharp eye on his or her accessories. Does his leather wallet sport a stitched-in cross? Does she keep a

For evangelicals, every fashion choice says, "I know Jesus, and you should too."

"JESUS LOVES YOU," BUT NOT ON WORK PHONE

MEMPHIS, TENN.—Mark Wubbeda, employee of Southern Micro Systems, used to answer the phone by saying, "Jesus loves you, this is Mark in tech support." Now he just says, "This is Mark in tech support."

"I'm not thrilled about hiding my witness, but I had to keep my job," says the 32-year-old computer programmer.

Mark's boss cracked down on him after receiving complaints from fellow employees who were offended by his insertion of religion into the workplace. Mark argued that "being a Christian is part of who I am in every sphere of life," and that since all his calls come from within the company, he should be free to express his religious views in a brief, non-intrusive way. But management disagreed.

"If we let him do it, then we'd have other religious things popping up," says general manager Dave Ekedy. "Can you imagine every time you called someone getting, 'Allah is great, this is Sandy,' or something? This is a tech company, not the council for world religions."

Mark also was forced to change his voice mail, which used to say, "This is Mark Wubbeda. Press one to hear a life-changing message of God's love." After a long pause it continued, "Press two to leave a message for Mark." Now a woman operator's voice simply says, "To leave a message for this recipient, please press one."

From LarkNews.com, a good source of Christian news

CLEVELAND-AREA REVIVAL ATTRIBUTED TO WOMAN'S SCRIPTURE CHECKS

CLEVELAND, OHIO—A citywide upswing in salvations and spiritual awareness is being credited to housewife Sandy Donadio's scripture checkbook.

Donadio ordered a box of flowery scripture checks in May and soon began using checks that read, "Trust in the Lord with all your heart," and, "I can do all things through Christ who strengthens me." Within days the city broke into revival.

"She left a trail of new converts behind her, at the 99 Cent store, Kroger, the auto shop, the dry cleaner," says one pastor whose congregation has grown by 30 percent. "I heard stories of grown men dropping to their knees right in public after receiving Donadio's payment. Thank God she ordered those checks."

A Bank of America bank teller says she dedicated her life to Christ after Donadio wrote a check for deposit. That check read, "I'll be like a tree planted by the water."

"I realized my need for a savior right then," says the teller. "My mom's been dunning me for years to go to church, but I had no desire until I read the special message in the corner of that check."

Donadio says she's so impressed with the unexpected results that she's ordering an extra box and plans to go on a shopping spree, "to fan the flames of revival in Cleveland."

From LarkNews.com, a good source of Christian news

small copy of the New Testament tucked in her purse? Is there a portrait of Raphael's cherubs on her Visa card? Does she have flowery scripture checks in her checkbook?

If the person in question is a co-worker, scan his or her workspace for spiritual knick-knacks. Do you see at least a dozen framed portraits of his family? Framed scripture verses on the walls? A Holy Land screen saver, or a Bible verse scrolling across the computer screen (for example, "I can do *all* things through Christ who strengthens *me!*")? A Women's Study Bible on the desk, *The Prayer of Jabez* set suggestively on the shelf, a copy of *Guideposts* magazine tossed oh-so-carelessly on the side table?

Take closer stock of the person's clothing and jewelry. Does he wear an IXOYE tie tack? A WWJD bracelet? Dog tags that identify him as belonging to the Lord's Army? Does she wear cross earrings? A dove broach?

After you gain confidence in identifying evangelicals in public, it will be time to take the next step and study them in their most preferred habitat: church.

Denomination pledges entire evangelism budget to converting Madonna

SPRINGFIELD, Mo. — The Assemblies of God denomination voted to spend $2.3 million — their entire 2007 evangelism budget — on converting Madonna.

"Dollar for dollar, it's a great plan," said spokesman Sean Taylor.

"If she gets saved, legions of fans will follow her."

The denomination will buy space on every billboard near the singer's homes in Los Angeles, New York and London. Billboards will bear messages like, "Spiritual girl — has a nice ring, doesn't it?" and "Madonna, Come to Jesus!" The denominati

Chapter 2
IDENTIFYING
EVANGELICALS IN
THE FIELD

Chapter 3

PLANNING YOUR FIELD TRIP TO AN EVANGELICAL CHURCH

Up to now you have watched evangelicals from afar. Now it's time to plunge fearlessly into their favorite habitat of all—church!—where you can observe the inner workings of evangelical community life.

CHOOSING A CHURCH

Your first order of business is to choose an evangelical church to attend. Grab the yellow pages and turn to "Houses of Worship." There you will find hundreds of listings. Narrow them down to evangelical churches by using these simple steps:

1. CROSS OFF ANY CHURCH NAMED AFTER A SAINT—THESE ARE CATHOLIC OR EPISCOPALIAN. Evangelicals never name churches after people because that would encourage self-aggrandizement. They believe that all "born-again" people are "saints" with the same status as St. Peter or St. Paul—good works notwithstanding—and they would no sooner name a church St. Peter's than they would name it St. Doug's.

2. CROSS OFF ANY CHURCH WITH AN ETHNIC DESIGNATION IN THE NAME. "Greek" or "Russian" means the church is Orthodox—ancient, highly ritualized, and hostile to evangelicals. "Ukrainian," "Korean," or "Armenian" indicates an evangelical church offering first-generation immigrants a worship experience like in the old country. The service probably wouldn't be in English, and your freebie might be a basket of boiled hen eggs.

3. CROSS OFF HOUSES OF WORSHIP WHOSE NAMES INCLUDE JEWISH WORDS AND THE WORD *TEMPLE*. These are Jewish temples. But watch out! "Bethel Temple" and "Calvary Temple" are common evangelical church names that only sound Jewish. *Beth-el* is Hebrew for "house of God." Calvary, of course, is what Christians call the hill where Jesus died. (*Note*: It's *Cal-vary*, not *cav-alry*. Jesus died on Calvary; he was not riding a horse.) Evangelicals borrow Jewish and Jewish-sounding terms for their meeting places because it makes them feel established. But cross off any "Bethel Temple" in your yellow pages anyway. It may be a Jewish temple, and even if it is a church, evangelicals should learn not to confuse people.

Evangelicals never name churches after people because it encourages self-aggrandizement. They would no sooner name a church St. Peter's than they would name it St. Doug's.

ARE MORMONS EVANGELICALS?

As an outraged evangelical might think but never say, "Hell, no." Though Mormons and evangelicals seem cut from the same cloth, they are highly antagonistic and competitive religions. Put an evangelical and a Mormon in a room and you would eventually have to call an ambulance or Dr. Phil.

Most evangelicals maintain a smug ignorance about Mormon theology. They sum it up like this:

a) Mormons believe in having multiple wives.

b) Mormons believe something about Jesus appearing to Native Americans and something about getting your own planet when you die.

c) Did we mention that multiple wives thing?

Evangelicals are threatened by the Mormons' ultra-successful evangelistic juggernaut, which is competing globally for souls. For their part, Mormons desperately wish to be seen as mainstream Christians, but evangelicals are having none of it.

4. CROSS OFF LISTINGS WITH ARABIC NAMES, LIKE AL AKBA AZAR OR AL BAQDA ISLAM. These are mosques. You will certainly not find evangelicals in them.

5. WHAT REMAIN IN YOUR PHONE BOOK ARE CHURCHES AND A SMATTERING OF OFF-BRAND RELIGIONS AND CHRISTIAN CULTS. Cross off names not entirely in English. This eliminates Sikh and Baha'i groups, and other patently un-evangelical religions. While you're at it, cross off Unitarian churches, which are

vehemently anti-evangelical, in their Bill Moyers–ish way. (Evangelicals have no clue what Unitarians believe, but they suspect them to be the religious arm of the Public Broadcasting System.)

6. CROSS OFF MORMON CHURCHES. They have similar habits, but very different theology (see sidebar).

7. CROSS OFF "KINGDOM HALLS," WHERE JEHOVAH'S WITNESSES MEET. Global membership of the Jehovah's Witnesses is growing rapidly, mostly on the strength of their glossy literature, but their beliefs are completely at odds with evangelicals'.

8. CROSS OFF CHRISTIAN SCIENCE CHURCHES, WHICH ARE NOT EVANGELICAL AND WOULD BE EMBARRASSED TO BE THOUGHT OF AS EVANGELICAL (THEY ARE, AFTER ALL, SCIENTISTS). Evangelicals feel no threat from Christian Science because the highly intellectual religion doesn't play well in Third World countries or the rural South, where evangelicals rule the roost. When was the last time you saw a Christian Science reading room in Tegucigalpa or next to a Steak & Shake?

9. NOW YOU WILL BE LEFT WITH CHURCHES WITH NAMES LIKE MAPLE AVENUE LUTHERAN, NEIGHBORHOOD METHODIST, AND THE LIKE. But you are looking for strictly evangelical churches, as opposed to mainline Protestant churches. "Mainline" means "politically liberal and declining precipitously in membership." Mainline churches include Lutherans, Methodists, Episcopalians, and Presbyterians.

To zero in on evangelical churches, here's the secret: circle any remaining house of worship whose name sounds like a drug or alcohol rehabilitation center or a home for troubled teens. You will end up with names like:

New Life Community

Hope Fellowship

The Lighthouse

Fountain of Life Family Center

Grace Community

If you investigate, you will find that these are not halfway houses at all, but actual, functioning evangelical churches. Why the elliptical names? To pique your curiosity and to advertise the gospel message with tact and a vague promise of comfort—similar to how laxatives are sold, without stating the purpose too bluntly. Evangelicals believe you are more likely to visit—and enjoy—a church that emphasizes life, grace, and hope as opposed to, say, death, burial, and resurrection.

An important footnote here: avoid churches that too proudly declare their affiliation with a specific denomination, such as "Louisville Assembly of God Church of the Assemblies of God" or "Tallahassee Southern Baptist Church, a Congregation of the Southern Baptist Convention." This means they are:

a) a handful of uneducated families;

b) legalistic to the point of obsession about some aspect of the denomination's theology; or

c) both.

Chapter 3
PLANNING YOUR
FIELD TRIP TO AN
EVANGELICAL
CHURCH

The same is true of any church that is so forward as to include the word *Bible* in its name (for example, Open Bible Church, Bible Baptist Church). These churches probably believe the Bible is being sorely neglected in the world *and* in other churches, and they probably view themselves as crusaders. Unless you enjoy sermons that amount to rallying cries to win the culture war, avoid these churches too.

You may now choose any church you have circled. Some will have quarter-page ads offering service times, directions, and a photo of the pastor. Or you may have to call the church office to get service times. Don't be afraid to do this! Make sure your caller ID is blocked, keep a list of evangelical phrases in a notebook on your lap (see chapter 6, "How to Talk and Act Like an Evangelical Without Being One"), and pretend you are passing through town on vacation. Get the information you need, offer a happy-sounding "God bless you," and hang up. If it makes you feel better, call from a pay phone.

MEGA-CHURCHES AND MINI-CHURCHES

Perhaps your city has a "mega-church," which some non-evangelicals spell "M-O-N-S-T-R-O-S-I-T-Y." Mega-churches are officially defined as churches with 2,000 or more people in weekly attendance, and they have earned a reputation for clogging up streets on Sunday mornings when perfectly happy agnostics are driving in their jammies to get the *Times* and a bagel. But on the global scene, U.S. mega-churches are veritable midgets. In Africa, Asia, and South America, churches routinely grow to tens of thousands of members, and a gathering of 2,000 Christians is considered a failed home Bible study.

The King of All Mega-Churches, Yoido Full Gospel Church in Seoul, Korea, has more than 500,000 members and operates its own newspaper and television station (it's true!). Imagine all of Oklahoma City's half-million residents raising their hands and belting out worship songs, and you get the picture.

Note: There are no mega-mosques or mega-synagogues in the United States. Nobody knows why, but evangelicals are very happy about it.

If your city is big enough and is not called "New York City," it probably has several mega-churches that offer a complete worship experience with the efficiency and scale of Costco, and about the same doughnut distribution. But if you become claustrophobic and snippy around hordes of evangelicals, skip the mega-church and head for a mini-church instead. Mini-churches draw fewer than 100 people and after years of bumping along have no expectation of growth. Like a dormant volcano, they have collapsed into nonthreatening inertness.

Mini-churches offer several benefits:

1. **Everybody knows everybody else.**

2. **You won't get lost in the facility.**

3. **They offer an environment where even the most mediocre work is welcomed and appreciated.**

4. **If you want to be the youth pastor, just ask.**

But mini-churches also offer several drawbacks:

1. **Everybody knows everybody else.**

2. **The facilities are often old and worn out.**

3. The pastor is usually lazy or terminally discouraged.

4. On your second visit they will ask you to serve as a board member.

Perhaps you would like to try both mega- and mini-churches, becoming a well-informed hobbyist. Take a few weeks and shop around, visiting churches of various sizes and noting their differences. By doing this, you will also be participating in a great evangelical tradition called "church-hopping." Church-hoppers attend a different church every week, sampling from the ecclesiastical smorgasbord but never committing to one place. This drives pastors absolutely insane but is a useful tactic for you, the curious observer.

CHOOSING THE SERVICE

The church you chose probably offers several services: one on Saturday night, several on Sunday morning, and perhaps one dying on the vine on Sunday night. Each service has its own "personality." Which should you attend? Let's compare.

Saturday Night

These services are a fairly recent innovation in evangelical churches, borrowed with considerable consternation from the Catholics. The pastor and worship team use Saturday service to fine-tune their performances. These services are shorter because they know they'll have to do it all again the next day.

Saturday evening services attract a variety of people, from those who want to dispense with their church obligation at the earliest opportunity to those who have important tasks to perform on Sunday morning, like sleeping till noon or watching football. They also draw that slice of the evangelical population that is so eager to hear the sermon they can't wait for Sunday morning. (Indeed, if they like it enough, they might attend Sunday morning too.)

Saturday evening services also tend to draw smaller crowds, so if you want to blend in, this is not your best choice. Neither does it represent the church at full throttle, so for your first visit you might skip this one.

First Service—aka "Early Service" or "Traditional Service"

In recent decades, evangelical worship time has become a generational battle between "Blessed Assurance" and "Rock Me, Jesus." Young believers prefer bouncy choruses with theologically sloppy lyrics and a backbeat; elderly believers want to sing all twenty-five verses of "Amazing Grace" (taking little naps in between) without the agitating presence of drums, electric guitars, and people under thirty-five.

Pastors and worship leaders have had a terrible time catering to both sides. They can't afford to alienate younger believers, who bring energy to a church, or older saints, who bring tithes and offerings. After aiming for complete unity—a nice biblical idea, but impractical—many pastors have opted for congregational mitosis and divided Sunday morning into two different services. First service has gone to the elderly.

If you are an early riser, or just enjoy hanging around with members of the Greatest Generation, attend a "first" or "traditional" service. They usually start between 7:00 A.M.

and 9:30 A.M. You will see women with "blue halos" and their slow-moving husbands wearing off-the-rack suits from 1975. You will hear the comforting strains of a church organ and observe how silver saints are relieved of the crushing burden of learning songs written after 1948. The pastor will preach quietly and without histrionics. He will not go longer than thirty minutes, or his audience may doze off and lack the vigor to drive home.

But you will not get the full evangelical church experience unless you attend second service.

Second Service—aka "Contemporary" Service

If you want to see an evangelical church at its pinnacle, attend second service on Sunday morning. It may be advertised as the "contemporary" service, because evangelicals know that "contemporary" is such a hot fashion buzzword among secular people.

At second service, any good evangelical church will be firing on all pistons. Sunday schools will be packed, the nursery rowdy and crying, the foyer buzzing. The pastor will know how to deliver his sermon for maximum comic and spiritual impact. People will come ready to applaud and praise. The worship team will be humming like a fine-tuned Italian race car. Or rather, like a recently winterized Ford Windstar.

The full second-service experience will be explored more in the next chapter.

Sunday Evening Service

This used to be evangelicals' signature meeting, the one that distinguished them from lukewarm Methodists and

Evangelicals increasingly dress down when congregating. Wearing less-expensive clothes also helps them convey how much money they are giving away to orphans and widows in Bangladesh.

Presbyterians who spent Sunday evenings listening to the radio or drinking hard liquor. At evangelical churches on Sunday evening, the pastor could preach longer, the people could "amen" louder, and the altar calls, particularly in Pentecostal churches, could get wackier.

But gradually evangelicals phased out these services because of their urgent need to watch *60 Minutes* and clip their toenails.

HOW TO DRESS

Evangelical fashion is governed by such a wide variety of customs that it is almost impossible to give useful recommendations about what to wear to church, but general rules do apply. Evangelicals used to dress up for church, back when people could only afford one nice suit, dress, and pair of shoes. Wearing your "Sunday clothes" was a way of telling God how important he was and of comparing your lovely hat and dress with the awful things your Christian friends chose to wear.

Nowadays, with the fortunate advent of cheap overseas child labor, people have lots of nice clothes and dressing up seems unnecessary. For this reason, evangelicals increasingly dress down when congregating. Wearing less-expensive clothes also helps them convey how much money they are giving away to orphans and widows in Bangladesh.

Unless you are attending a church event in the South, don't wear fancy clothes. Aim instead for the broad middle of the fashion road. If you are a man, wear Dockers and a business shirt (no tie) or a Polo shirt. Don't wear a T-shirt with a brash Christian slogan. Church is

Chapter 3
PLANNING YOUR FIELD TRIP TO AN EVANGELICAL CHURCH

the wrong place to make evangelistic statements. These T-shirts work well, however, for Friday night street witnessing and for high schoolers actively seeking persecution from their peers.

If you are a woman, wear a pantsuit rather than a dress. If you wear a dress, other evangelicals will think you are making a subtle statement about the immorality of pants. Or they will guess that you didn't do laundry all week.

Don't dress down to the point of wearing shorts and T-shirts, unless you live in California, Florida, or Hawaii. In these casual states, you are considered "dressed up" if you wear anything more than sandals, shorts, and a Hawaiian flower-print shirt. (If you wear slacks there, you might hear, "See you got your long pants on there, Bill. What's the occasion?")

Before you head out your door, practice your confident smile in the mirror. Evangelicals are keenly attuned to spiritual uncertainty, like sharks to the smell of blood. Once they think you are a sinner in need of salvation, you will attract unwanted attention. But if you simply appear to be a savvy evangelical visitor from another city, they will let you skate through without interference. Indeed, they will want to impress you at every turn.

Also, take care of your personal hygiene. You will be in close quarters with these people for an hour or two (or three if there is a guest evangelist). Be generous with the deodorant and bring breath mints.

Now that you've chosen your church, your service, and your clothing, it's time for the field trip. Set your alarm for Sunday morning—let's go to church!

Chapter 4

ARRIVING AT CHURCH

This is the big day! You are about to venture into the heart of the evangelical community and witness their most important spiritual exercises up close. But before you go, choose your "visitor strategy":

COVERT MISSION—**You can try to fly under the radar and remain perfectly anonymous throughout your visit, but evangelical churches are so eager for new members that someone will undoubtedly ask, "Are you new here?" The smaller the church, the more likely it is that your presence will cause a stir.**

KING FOR A DAY—**In evangelical churches, complete strangers who show up on Sunday morning are often feted and befriended from the**

The foyer will be filled with jokey, back-slapping, neck-hugging Christians of all shapes and sizes (trending round).

moment they step into the foyer. If you need a refreshing break from the harsh workaday world, you might want to declare up front that you are a first-time visitor and receive the special attention that member-hungry evangelicals are ready to bestow on you.

ARRIVING

Plan to arrive fifteen minutes early to explore the facility and observe pre-service socialization rituals. You won't have any trouble parking, as most evangelical churches have special sections for first-time visitors. Tell the volunteer parking attendants—those happy fellows in orange vests—that you are a first-time visitor, and they will direct you to parking spaces tucked up against the church building. This will save you from running the gauntlet of minivans in the parking lot.

As you walk toward the front entrance of the church, assume a look of joy and expectation. Other families will do the same, even though most of them will have fought like badgers on the way to church. Most evangelical families save their best pouts and surliest attitudes for Sunday mornings. They blame this on the devil, who wants to rob them of their weekly worship experience.

As you approach the building, you may hear loud, raucous noises emanating from it. Don't worry. This only means that the people are engaging in "praise and worship." (Or, if the sounds are intensely ecstatic, perhaps John Ashcroft has just entered the building.) The two things evangelicals do in unity and strength are sing and vote. You are about to see them do the first.

Stationed at each entrance to the church will be greeters who smile at you as you walk in. Their job is not to convert you, and they do not intend to have a long inter-action with you. Rather, they function as a church's on-site Welcome Committee (remember the Wal-Mart greeters?). In their hands will be a stack of bulletins. As you draw within a few feet of them, they will give you one and per-haps shake your hand. If you seem confused, they will offer to escort you to your desired location or hail an usher to help you.

Ushers are the men in matching coats stationed throughout the facility. They have roughly the same job as theater ushers. They help people find seats, pass out the offering plates, and beat the daylights out of you if you make a move toward the pastor. (It's a post–9/11 world. Churches are tense.) Many ushers are guys who fancy they could have had brilliant careers as cops/sheriffs/bouncers/mafia hit men.

Near the entrance there may be an information desk arrayed with Christian literature and staffed by contented-looking women. They are well trained to spot newcomers, so if you wish to remain anonymous for now, don't make eye contact with them. Rather, smile broadly and survey the room with the confidence of an evangelical waiting for her spouse to park the car.

Having passed them by, you are now in the center of the foyer, the crossroads of the evangelical social experi-ence. It will be filled with jokey, back-slapping, neck-hugging Christians of all shapes and sizes (trending round). The roar of conversation and the cacophony of perfumes and colognes will give it a heady air, like opening night at a Broadway play. Navigate your way to a safe corner and

Chapter 4
ARRIVING
AT CHURCH

observe for a while. You will see men, women, and children toting Bibles of every imaginable size and shape, some of them brand-new, some old and beat-up from years of diligent study. The room will be decked with silk plants and inoffensive watercolor art. You won't see statues, as they smack of Catholicism and modern art museums. On the wall there may be a rack of gospel tracts, information about local ministries, or voter guides for the upcoming election, all free for the taking.

Soak in the electricity of the moment and feel the crackle of anticipation as the evangelicals around you prepare for their worship experience. This is the buildup to the main event they have been looking forward to all week.

THE SELF-GUIDED TOUR

Before the service begins, give yourself a quick tour of the facility. Saunter down the hallways and watch Sunday school teachers prepping their crafts and writing memory verses on the boards. See nursery workers setting out toys and wiping spit-up off the rocking chairs. Smell the scent of fresh coffee and Krispy Kreme doughnuts that permeates the Sunday school wing, driving evangelicals to delirium.

Peek into various rooms and see the choir rehearsing, ushers preparing the Communion elements, and, if you are at a mini-church in West Virginia, people dancing around with rattlesnakes.

If you are in a mega-church, you may want to order breakfast at the McDonald's in the foyer. Some churches also offer bookstores, where you may purchase everything from Christian comic books to IXOYE neckties. If you

If you are in a mega-church, you may want to order breakfast at the McDonald's in the foyer.

USHERS WITH STUN GUNS STIR CONTROVERSY

MONTGOMERY, ALA.—Ron Henning recalls the day he first "put a man down" in the center aisle just before the pastor gave the altar call.

"I thought he was reaching for a weapon in his pocket," Henning says. He zapped the man with a church-issued stun gun and sent him to the floor, throwing the service into tumult. It turned out the man was heading to the altar to give his heart to Christ. The church apologized and paid the man $500, but he has not returned.

"Mix-ups happen, but there are crazies out there who might try to take out the man on the platform," says head usher Tim O'Daley.

First Baptist Church has gone further than most to protect its congregation, outfitting the entire usher crew with high-powered stun guns.

"It feels good," says O'Daley, patting the holster concealed under his usher jacket.

Jake Fitzgerald, 18, was zapped when he got up to use the restroom during the sermon. The jolt was so powerful that he "forgot I was on planet Earth," he says.

"There's an invisible line, and when people cross it, we pounce," says O'Daley unapologetically.

Fitzgerald recovered in a back room and was released, with a free copy of the sermon on tape. He now sits in the back row on Sunday mornings and never flinches.

The ushers practice their drills monthly, tackling dummies and leaping over pews. They have yet to confront a real malefactor. That doesn't mean they aren't ready.

"I can get the gun out in less than 1.5 seconds," O'Daley says, demonstrating proudly.

From LarkNews.com, a good source of Christian news

Chapter 4
ARRIVING
AT CHURCH

have time, play a little game: try to find a single item in the store that is not stamped with a Bible verse. *Hint:* you won't, not even among the breath mints.

THE NURSERY

If you have brought your children to church with you—a very evangelical thing to do—you may drop them off at the nursery. If you have no children but are intent on blending in, borrow the children of a friend. Tell her that church nurseries are a terrific place for kids to learn character-building stories and pick up the latest strain of influenza.

If you are a tuckered-out parent, you can plan for future Sundays full of child-free rest. Churches offer one to two hours of free child care per service to anyone who shows up. If a church has three morning services, you could drop your kids off at 8:00 A.M. and pick them up at 2:00 P.M., and nobody would ask questions. Strictly speaking, the child care is for people attending the church. But perhaps you commune best with God while getting your hair done at the mall or reading the newspaper in bed. These places become "church" to you. Having removed any residual guilt (an evangelical concept borrowed wholesale from the Catholics), you may find your weekends revolutionized by the free child care offered by church nurseries.

Here are strategies for using church nurseries as free child care:

1. **Arrive during the "crush," which begins fifteen minutes before the service starts and tapers off about ten minutes into it. Checking**

in during the busiest time may seem inconvenient, but it ensures the longevity of your strategy. If you rush in half an hour late, you'll only attract suspicion.

2. Adopt the manner of someone who is late for her spot in the choir.

3. Don't wear sweats and have your hair up in a ponytail. Look presentable, or your fiction will fall apart.

With careful coordination, your weekend schedule might look like this:

SATURDAY EVENING, 6:00 TO 7:30 P.M.—**Candlelight dinner with husband. Kids at Evangelical Free Church.**

SUNDAY MORNING, 8:30 A.M. TO NOON—**"Me" time. Go out for a smoothie. Take in a movie. Kids at Family Christian Center (all three services).**

SUNDAY EVENING, 6:15 TO 11:00 P.M.—**Work out at gym. Sushi dinner and a nice long bath. Kids at Pentecostal Holiness Church revival meeting.**

THE EVANGELICAL SOCIAL CALENDAR

Before service is a good time to review the bulletin you received at the door. Bulletins are useful repositories of church information that include an urgent plea for nursery workers and a welcome note from the pastor, with a picture of him and his wife looking happily married indeed.

Bulletins also spell out a church's doctrines (look for a "What We Believe" section).

Most important, the bulletin contains the church calendar, which is tantamount to the evangelical social calendar. Since they don't go to taverns or most movies, evangelicals keep their own busy social schedule, which helps to keep their minds off what they're missing. Evangelical church calendars are bursting with men's breakfasts, ladies' brunches, prayer meetings, youth outings, couples' retreats, craft fairs, potlucks, and Friday night screenings of *The Passion of the Christ: Director's Cut* in the fellowship hall.

If you dive wholeheartedly into the evangelical social scene, your weekly calendar could be crammed with activities like these:

Women's Bible study

Friday Night Alive! youth meeting

Men's breakfast

Ladies' brunch

Baseball game

Fishing trip

Couples' retreat at Tablerock Lake Hotel and Spa

Singles' group water ski trip

Prayer meeting

Church work day

Best of all, as a "newcomer," you will get into each of these events for free.

Having tasted the pre-service atmosphere and satisfied your curiosity with a tour of the facility, follow the sound of music and conversation into the main room of the church, the sanctuary, where the most important 90 to 120 minutes of the evangelical week are about to begin.

CHURCH BULLETIN HISTORY

The first church bulletin ever discovered was handwritten on goatskin. It contained a schedule of service times and an urgent plea for nursery workers.

In medieval times, bulletins were laboriously copied on parchment by embittered youth pastors working by candlelight.

Today, some churches zap the bulletin to people's PDAs when they arrive at church.

Chapter 4
**ARRIVING
AT CHURCH**

THE EVANGELICAL CHURCH SERVICE

Welcome to an evangelical church service! Whether you chose a small corner church or a mega-center with reclining theater seats and a Jumbotron, the service will offer nearly identical features: praise and worship time, a sermon, and five opportunities to give money. Going in, you may think that evangelical services are loosey-goosey, seat-of-your-pants affairs. Not true. You will soon find their services are as ritualized and predictable as the 10,047th performance of *Les Misérables*.

If you are nervous about the whole enterprise, imagine that when you walk into the sanctuary you have wandered instead into a community theater presentation. The worship band is the slightly off-key volunteer orchestra. The pastor is a well-meaning but tragic King Lear giving his soliloquy on the rain-battered heath. The associate pastor is Macbeth, plotting his ascent. The pastor's wife is Ophelia, melancholy and depressed. The youth pastor is Bobby Brady.

Let's watch as the curtain goes up.

GETTING THROUGH WORSHIP TIME WITHOUT INCIDENT

You may sit anywhere you please in an evangelical church, but certain seats send a signal. Front-row sitters are expected to be enthusiastic worshipers. (And you'd have to turn around to observe everyone, which would be impolite.) Back-row sitters are usually down-on-their-luck backsliders or people with weak bladders—both want quick access to the exit in case their fortitude fails. To attract the least attention, sit in the middle row and casually flip through your bulletin.

The service begins with "praise and worship." The worship team will emerge from backstage and may consist of one person or two hundred, depending on the church's talent pool and the worship leader's ambition. Aside from the worship leader, all musicians and singers are volunteers. Their performance may reflect this. Here are some common worship team styles you might see, classified by their resemblance to popular types of Broadway stage shows:

UP WITH PEOPLE—A phalanx of enthusiastic singers assaults you with cheer from the edge of the platform. Backing them up is a full choir and orchestra playing tightly choreographed and upbeat songs. Their task: energize and inspire. You *will* be happy.

You are now witnessing evangelicals' most important time of community bonding and expression. In worship they achieve the same state of collective bliss teens experience at a rock concert or Manhattanites experience at the latest Tony Kushner play.

"TOMMY"—Rock- or grunge-style worship. Signals a young church desperate for respect from mainstream pop culture.

"HAIR" —A motley group of flautists, percussionists, singers, and women in ankle-length hemp dresses make up this loose ensemble. Listen for Jethro Tull—style flute solos and extended "praise jams." Common at smallish charismatic churches.

ONE-MAN SHOW—A lone, sensitive guy on guitar or piano leads worshipers on an exploration of his ever-widening emotional landscape, via song. An odyssey of spiritual interiors.

BOX-OFFICE FLOP—When the pastor, his wife, or both lead worship, it's a sign of the church's impending bankruptcy and the pastoral couple's imminent nervous breakdowns.

No matter what the style, when worship starts, people will stand up. You will suddenly be surrounded by noisy, clapping, singing evangelicals. At this point in mini-churches in West Virginia, they'll bring out the snakes.

You are now witnessing evangelicals' most important time of community bonding and expression. In worship they achieve the same state of collective bliss teens experience at a rock concert or Manhattanites experience at the latest Tony Kushner play. After holding their breath all week and suffering the world's slings and arrows, evangelicals let out the pent-up pressure with a collective shout on Sunday morning.

Fast songs always come first, then midtempo numbers, then "Freebird." Most churches display the song lyrics on screens, so feel free to mouth along. Also, remain standing throughout worship time. When someone sits down early, it means he or she is fat or pregnant or thinks worship time has gone too long. No need to draw attention to yourself by sitting.

You may notice people around you lifting their hands and singing with abandon. Unless they are bumping your head, you'll have to live with this. It didn't bother you at the REO Speedwagon concert at the county fair. It shouldn't bother you here. Rather, take the opportunity to observe the worship styles around you. Notice how that conservative gentleman in his fifties burst to life and began jumping, singing, and pumping his fists in the air. Watch the elegant woman turn circles and wave her hands in the air like a wayward ballerina. Watch the teenage girl kneel and weep in the aisle as if she just lost her puppy. Anything goes during evangelical worship time, as long as someone's not getting their groove on with sensual nightclub moves.

For evangelicals, the sanctuary is a safe place where they shed public mannerliness and celebrate their faith without fear of criticism. What happens in the sanctuary stays in the sanctuary. And even if they appear foolish, who cares? They are worshiping the God who gave them life, gave them salvation, gave them the White House and Congress. He is worthy of praise.

The quality of worship time is so important that it sets the mood for evangelicals' entire week. If worship time is too short or less-than-ecstatic, disappointed evangelicals find themselves in a funk by Wednesday. You might hear

COMMON HAND-
RAISING POSTURES

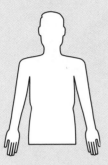

Low and Open

The Mime

One-handed
Surrender

One-handed
Point

Two-handed
Surrender

Two-handed
Point

HAND-RAISING SYMBOLS

Here are the universal symbols for "hand-raising permitted" and "hand-raising not permitted," which many churches post in the foyer:

them say, "What an awful week. Worship time on Sunday was terrible, and things just went downhill from there."

Many non-evangelicals wonder, "Do they expect me to raise my hands too?" No. But if you feel conspicuous by not participating, adopt an expression of deep reflection and grip the seat in front of you. Your worshiping neighbors will think you are so consumed by the presence of God that you would lose your balance by raising your hands. Or, if you like, close your eyes and imagine you are in the front row at a Rolling Stones concert. Sway, sing, and enjoy the cathartic release, but don't hold up your lighter or the ushers will give you the bum's rush.

As the worship team barrels along, the worship leader may exhort the audience with certain phrases:

"GIVE THE LORD A CLAP OFFERING"—This is not a request for money or (for the benefit of low-minded readers) an oblique reference to venereal disease. It refers to group applause for God. If a worship leader says this, everyone will

POLL RESULTS

I Raise My Hands In Worship

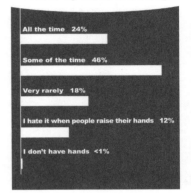

All the time **24%**

Some of the time **46%**

Very rarely **18%**

I hate it when people raise their hands **12%**

I don't have hands **<1%**

HELPFUL HEADLINE

WORSHIP LEADER CLOSES EYES, FORGETS WHERE HE IS

SAN ANTONIO, TEX.—Jim Taylor, 35, the worship leader at Full Gospel Tabernacle, closed his eyes during worship Sunday morning and forgot where he was. The result, witnesses say, was twenty minutes of same-chord strumming that left the audience baffled.

"He kind of faded out, but he had this big smile on his face, so we thought he was enjoying the presence of the Lord," says one witness.

Taylor said afterward that during the worship service he began to think he was in his bedroom playing his guitar.

"During the week I sit on my bed and play guitar for hours," he says. "I'm just glad I opened my eyes after twenty minutes and realized I was in church."

Some people began to leave after ten minutes. Even more left after Jim began jamming on the Beatles' "Day Tripper," during which he sang alternately harmony and melody. His eyes were still closed at that point.

"I left him alone," says the senior pastor when asked why he didn't intervene. "I hire people and trust them to do their job. I'm surprised he forgot where he was, but some people were blessed by it."

From LarkNews.com, a good source of Christian news

Chapter 5
THE EVANGELICAL CHURCH SERVICE

WORSHIP LEADER'S
WORK SCHEDULE

MONDAY—Day off

TUESDAY—Think of what songs to play on Sunday

WEDNESDAY—Think of what songs to play on Sunday

THURSDAY—Think of what songs to play on Sunday

FRIDAY—Think of what songs to play on Sunday

SATURDAY—Day off

SUNDAY—Play songs

clap in the direction of the ceiling. It will last twenty seconds or less, unless people get to whooping.

"FOCUS ON THE LORD"—Translation: Quit thinking about the football/basketball/NASCAR event you're missing on television.

"LIFT HIM UP"—Translation: Sing louder.

"ENTER IN"—Translation: The music is slowing down, so surrender to a relaxed, trancelike state of praise so no one around you feels embarrassed for being in the same relaxed, trancelike state.

How long will worship time last? Here's a convenient chart:

Church Type	Duration
Seeker-friendly (see glossary)	It's not worship; it's the opening song set
Methodist	5 minutes
Southern Baptist	12 to 15 minutes
Charismatic	45 to 60 minutes
Pentecostal churches in Alabama	Whenever Sister Hilda quits rolling around

HE'S NUMBER TWO—AND THAT'S OKAY

After worship is finished and people are pleasantly pooped, the associate pastor—the church's humble second fiddle—steps briefly into the spotlight to give the announcements. This gives him an opportunity to bond with the people with a few lighthearted jokes he spent all week crafting. Like any second-in-command, he must also show a bit of leadership mettle. After all, he's only a heartbeat away from the pulpit.

Most churches have done away with the tradition of guest torture called "acknowledging the first-time visitors," but it still pops up, especially in congregations that advertise themselves as "The Friendly Church!" The associate pastor may invite first-time visitors to stand while everyone else applauds them. If you stand, you will be besieged with promises of everlasting friendship, and the ushers will give you a welcome packet that may include a church pen,

HELPFUL HEADLINE

PASTOR WARY OF ASSOCIATE'S MOTIVES

GROTON, CONN.—Pastor Leo Thompson of Grace Community Church has begun to worry that the associate he hired three years ago is trying to win over the church, one announcement at a time.

"I gave him the task of giving Sunday morning announcements," Thompson says, "but he drags it out with lots of jokes and gives a mini-sermon with outline. By the time I take the podium, the people are tired out."

The associate pastor, Dennis Murray, denies using the announcements to angle for a bigger role.

"Me? Envious of the pastor? Heh-heh, nosiree," Murray says, taking a break from his painstaking work on next Sunday's announcements and sermonette. "I'm happy to be the number-two man. Not a word of complaint here."

Asked why his announcements now run more than fifteen minutes long on Sundays, he says he wants to give Thompson "a good run-up." Murray recently began offering a tape series of his best announcements via a high-end personal ministry website. "Highlights from the Announcements 2003," a ten-tape series, has sold 150 copies, he says.

"People like the jokes, I guess," he says, downplaying the popularity. The tapes, he says, are "absolutely meant to supplement the sermon tapes Pastor Thompson is offering."

Thompson has twice canceled a vacation because he worries about giving Murray too much face time with the people. But recently Murray took up a surprise offering to send Thompson and his wife to Bermuda for eight days—and two Sundays—to celebrate their nineteenth wedding anniversary.

"Nineteen is a very special milestone," says Murray, who will be preaching both weekends the Thompsons are away.

From LarkNews.com, a good source of Christian news

mug, refrigerator magnet, and a new convert handbook, which you can use to prop up that table leg or as a gag gift for your irreligious friend. If you don't stand, people will stare at you and wonder, "Why isn't he standing? I've never seen him here before." There is no good way out of this.

After the announcements, the tithes and offerings will be received. A tithe is a tenth of what you earn (gambling winnings too). An offering is money given freely above the tithe. Tithes and offerings are usually collected by ushers who pass a plate or bag down each row or hold members by their ankles and shake them until their wallets drop out.

ASSOCIATE PASTOR'S WORK SCHEDULE

MONDAY—Wipe down urinals; gather up used tissues and bulletins in sanctuary

TUESDAY—Empty Diaper Genies in nursery wing; sanitize

WEDNESDAY—Work on "sermons I'd give if I had the chance" project

THURSDAY—Wash pastor's golf balls

FRIDAY—Drop off pastor's dry cleaning; visit dying elderly

SATURDAY—On-call for counseling

SUNDAY—Give announcements

If you want to participate but don't want to actually give, take a tithe envelope from the seat pocket in front of you, pretend to slip a check into it, and drop it in the offering plate. If your neighbors are especially snoopy, write VOID on a check, black out your name, fold it in half, and drop it in with evident satisfaction.

It is impolite to ask how much other people tithe. The only people who know are the pastor, his secretary, who records it in the church books, and the secretary's husband, neighbors, interested friends, and acquaintances about town.

Where does your tithe money go? Where you might expect:

TO PAY THE LEASE on the church facility and the pastor's Lexus

TO HUSH UP EXTRAMARITAL LOVERS (applies primarily to leaders of major television ministries)

TO PAY FOR THE COMMUNION ELEMENTS—you think grape juice and saltines are free?

While the tithes and offerings are received (or taken), many churches allow a soloist to perform a song. Welcome to the *Desperate Housewives* portion of the service when, after practicing for weeks in her car, a woman with a painful lack of talent also demonstrates her inability to evaluate her own skill sets. When she's finished dissecting your inner cortex with her tongue and everyone applauds, she'll point to heaven, blaming God for her voice.

Welcome to the *Desperate Housewives* portion of the service when, after practicing for weeks in her car, a woman with a painful lack of talent also demonstrates her inability to evaluate her own skill sets.

This brings us to the most dangerous man in the building: the sound man. A disgruntled sound man can turn a service into a disaster for everyone involved. He can produce ear-splitting feedback with the flick of a wrist, cut the pastor's mic in and out and ruin the sermon, kill the monitors so the worship team loses their key, or crank the pitch knob up so the soloist dissolves into tears upon failing to reach that climactic note.

The sound man might give you a good time, if he's in the mood and you slip him a twenty.

THE PASTOR'S WIFE

By now you may be wondering: who is that woman on the front row smiling to beat the band? She is the pastor's wife, and if anyone in this melodrama deserves your pity, it is she. A pastor's wife is a tragic character, constrained by evangelical tradition from having a career, but not allowed to have authority in the church, lest she be labeled "controlling" by church members who think she's a Lady Macbeth. A pastor's wife can't share her true feelings with church members because that would shame her husband. And other pastors' wives in town treat her cattily.

BE A PEN PAL FOR A PASTOR'S WIFE

Are you willing to lend an ear to a pastor's wife who needs someone to dump on? Do you have a high tolerance for stories of church-related intrigue? The Pen Pal for a Pastor's Wife (PPPW) program pairs pastors' wives with sympathetic correspondents in other cities. Befriend a needy pastor's wife today!

PASTOR'S WIFE SENDS BODY DOUBLE TO SIT PLEASANTLY ON FRONT PEW

GRAND FORKS, MICH.—Unbeknownst to her husband or congregation, Trudy Smith has been avoiding church for two years, sending a look-alike in her place.

"I'm saddened to announce that the woman you've seen here is not my wife," pastor Nevin Smith said to a hushed congregation at Belfrey Presbyterian Church.

His wife Trudy began staying home after running into a woman at Kohl's who looked very much like her.

"I asked what she did on Sunday mornings, and would she like to make a hundred bucks a week?" Trudy says. "She said yes, and suddenly I was free."

The impostor played the role successfully, greeting people, hugging her husband, and taking copious sermon notes. But she was found out when Nevin invited her up one Sunday for a spontaneous reprisal of an old hymn they had sung early in their ministry.

"I knew the kids' names, anniversaries, and birthdays, but I didn't know that song," says the fake Trudy, who asked not to be identified. She made roughly $10,000 over two years.

"Worth every penny," says the real Trudy, who's back on the front pew. "You know, mannequins are getting more realistic...."

From LarkNews.com, a good source of Christian news

Stuck in a netherworld of crafting and women's ministry teas, pastors' wives cope by reminding themselves of God's wonderful plan for their lives and by having adulterous affairs. They also find solace in raising their children, the "PKs," or pastor's kids, so well known in evangelical circles for being model students who never raise hell or run off with their pregnant girlfriends.

THE MAIN ATTRACTION

It's now time for the sermon, a profound collection of ideas that occurred to the pastor between the twelfth and thirteenth holes on the golf course Saturday afternoon.

Note: If your pastor is a woman, you are not in an evangelical church but some kind of mainline church or real estate seminar.

The sermon is the high point of the pastor's job and determines his emotional health for the week to come. He wants to entertain, enlighten, and convict his audience. To this end, he may use clever methods to make his sermon more effective:

POWERPOINT PRESENTATION—**When a pastor acts like Bill Gates at a shareholder meeting, with PowerPoint slides popping up to accompany each of his points, it probably means his true calling is to middle management.**

ACROSTICS—**Pastors sometimes think people are too flaky to remember the sermon points unless the first letter of each point spells out a word, creating a helpful acrostic, like so:**

Church splits over spelling of 'hallelujah'

GREELEY — A little Jewish praise word caused a lot of controversy as a Colorado church, divided over the proper spelling of 'hallelujah,' split into separate congregations.

"It makes a tremendous difference," said a hallelujah supporter. "It's so jarring to see it without the 'h'. Nobody spells it that way anymore."

"I was so sick about it I couldn't sleep," said Evelyn Haney, 57, an equally ardent "alleluia" supporter. "To think some people spell this wonderful word with a 'j' in it. It's not something where I question their salvation, but at times you have to wonder."

The two churches now mee

WOMAN WINS LOTTERY, LEAVES TOWN WITHOUT TITHING

HOBOKEN, N.J.—Martha Givens, a faithful member of Walnut Methodist Church, won the $89 million New Jersey state lottery Tuesday, then left town, surprising her longtime pastor, Duane Marshall.

"I guess the right words would be 'deeply disappointed,'" Marshall says. Immediately after the news of Givens's winning broke, he and the board had hired an architectural firm to build a new multimillion-dollar youth center. As a church of 124, Walnut Methodist couldn't build the youth center without Givens's tithe from the lottery winnings.

"Martha's been so consistent through the years, we felt this was money in the bank," says a board member. "But I warned them she might turn tail. Eighty-nine million is a lot of money."

Family members are keeping mum about Givens's whereabouts, though word leaked that she is "somewhere in the Caribbean, hitting the senior singles bars, and doing all sorts of things Methodists don't do."

A sign on Givens's lawn indicates the house is for sale, and her front door is covered with "call me" notes from old friends and acquaintances.

Pastor Marshall hasn't given up hope she'll return—and tithe.

"Martha, if you read this, we'll take five percent, one percent, whatever you'll give," he says. "The Martha Givens Youth Center won't be a reality without you."

From LarkNews.com, a good source of Christian news

L-et others know how you feel about them.

O-wn up to your feelings.

V-olunteer to give hugs and affection.

E-arn people's love in return.

Or,

U-nderstand your calling.

S-ay yes to God.

U-se the abilities he gave you.

C-all on him during hard times.

K-eep going!

GREEK AND HEBREW OVERLOAD—**Some pastors justify their seminary education and whopping student loans by endlessly defining Bible words in the original Greek and Hebrew. This often mystifies evangelical listeners, who know the Bible was originally written in King James English.**

MOVIE CLIPS—**Pastors desperate to be "relevant" use movie clips as jumping-off points for their sermons. If a pastor does this, there is a high probability he also wears a goatee and sports the latest hip look in eyeglasses.**

A pastor may preach on any topic he pleases. Once in the pulpit, he no longer has to answer to a cranky board, a Prozac-addled wife, or an increasingly surly associate pastor. If you don't like his choice of topics, remember the words of Jesus to Peter: "Tough titty" (John 21:18). Nobody dragged you here, there was no cover charge, and even if you gave in the offering, that's God's money now.

Chapter 5
THE EVANGELICAL
CHURCH SERVICE

Sermons last from twenty to sixty minutes. To pass the time more quickly you may imagine it as a piece of avant-garde performance art that ironically combines a dramatic monologue, a motivational speech, and a time-share pitch to demonstrate the absurdity of modern culture. Invent review blurbs in your head like, "wickedly subversive" and "painfully hilarious." You may get more out of it than the people around you who are convinced he's speaking a straightforward message on perseverance.

Speaking of time-share pitches, the sermon will end with an altar call. The pastor will invite people to raise their hands if they would like to be saved. During this time you must remain absolutely motionless. The pastor—or "auctioneer," if you like—will scan the auditorium looking for any twitch indicating he has convinced someone to take the spiritual leap into evangelical Christianity. If you dare to scratch your head, you may become the church's latest convert. It would embarrass everyone when you admit you can't stay for new believers' class because you're meeting the guys at the pool hall.

If the sermon has gone over time, the pastor may remark that he hears "tummy clocks ticking," and he'll promise that you will still beat the other churches to the restaurants. If you've hosted successful parties, you know it's hard to let the guests go when you're having so much fun. Be a dear—let him have his moment. After all, on Monday morning he will wake up depressed and blame himself for even the tiniest misstep he committed on Sunday, a syndrome pastors call the Monday Morning Blues.

You are very close to getting out of your church experience alive and unconverted. When the pastor dismisses the service, the people will gather in the foyer and con-

The pastor—or "auctioneer," if you like—will scan the auditorium looking for any twitch indicating he has convinced someone to take the spiritual leap into evangelical Christianity. If you dare to scratch your head, you may become the church's latest convert.

gratulate one another with phrases like, "Wasn't that a terrific sermon?" and, "Worship today was awesome." Walk
briskly to your car with a look of complete fulfillment. As
you drive out of the parking lot, maintain ultimate cour-
tesy. Smile and wave at other drivers. Honking is disal-
lowed except for a quick toot-and-wave that conveys,
"Had a great time! Can't wait for next Sunday!" If other
drivers seem impatient with you, keep in mind that you are
between them and Shoney's.

Congratulations! You have completed your first field
trip to an evangelical church. To help you avoid awk-
wardly fumbling through the post-sermon socializing, the
next chapter will introduce you to the conversational
techniques you can use in the presence of evangelicals so
as to seem like "one of them."

Chapter 5
THE EVANGELICAL
CHURCH SERVICE

HOW TO TALK AND ACT LIKE AN EVANGELICAL WITHOUT BEING ONE

Evangelicals are everywhere, and if you wish to thrive in modern workplaces and social environments, you must learn to emulate and fraternize with them so convincingly that they don't realize you're an impostor. This chapter teaches you how to mingle with evangelicals in any circumstance or venue. It also offers a cheat sheet to help you fake it through a typical evangelical-style conversation.

Don't order anything that must be qualified with the word *virgin*, particularly a "virgin Mary," which flagrantly offends.

GREETING, DRINKING, AND EATING

When you find yourself among evangelicals in any location, offer a standard greeting, coupled with a phrase like "God is good" or "Praise God" or "What a blessing." Give a warm handshake, perhaps pulled into a brief hug if the person is of the same gender. If the person is of a different gender, make brief, friendly eye contact, then look away so as not to show untoward interest. If the person has intentionally obscured his or her gender, or is a cross-dresser or transvestite, you are not among evangelicals at all but are probably in a hotel bar in San Francisco.

If you happen to be with evangelicals in a "secular" location like a restaurant or airport, avoid alcoholic drinks and drinks with suggestive or celebrity-derived names. You may enjoy a Coors Cutter, Shirley Temple, or Roy Rogers on your own time, but not here. Also, don't order anything that must be qualified with the word *virgin*, particularly a "virgin Mary," which flagrantly offends. To order a virgin version of anything shows too much familiarity with the bar and might lead impressionable evangelicals into abject alcoholism.

You may eat anything you wish in as great a quantity as you wish. Excessive eating is not considered too terrible of a sin. It might even be godly, as the Bible specifically says that the righteous "shall be fat and flourishing" (Psalms 92:14). Do, however, apologize for eating continually, joke about your spare tire, and mention that you're "built for comfort, not for speed." Then take a moment to observe the overeating evangelicals around you; it is one of the few chances you will have to see them behaving wrongly on purpose and relishing it.

STARTING CONVERSATION

The initial conversation will center on your church and city. Your questioner will say, "Tell me about your church," or perhaps, "What's God doing in your city?"

The appropriate response is:

1. **"There is unprecedented unity among churches."**

2. **"We're spending lots of time in prayer."**

3. **"We're working hard to evangelize the city."**

The more you talk about the increase in these three things, the more deeply moved and affirmed your listener

CHURCH SIZE MATTERS

Evangelicals are highly competitive about church size. Some churches calculate their size by the number of people who attend on Sunday morning. Others count all the people they "touch" in any given week, including those visited in the hospital, those sent bulk mailings, and those prayed for. It is easy for a church of 100 to claim thousands of members by spreading itself around a bit.

Baptist churches are particularly adept at this. They define a member as any person, alive or dead, who visited the church once in the past thirty years, plus all of his or her relatives, whose existence need not be verified. For this reason, Southern Baptists, a group of about 21,000 nationwide, have long boasted the largest membership of any Protestant denomination, about 15 million. That muffled sound you hear is dead Baptists in their graves applauding their membership superiority.

will be. He or she may even hug you out of pure excitement.

Also note that the question "Tell me about your church" should be construed as a mannerly way of asking how large your church is. Size matters to evangelicals. But because you don't really attend church, "your church" can be as large as you want. Here are some tips.

Avoid saying you belong to a mini-church. If you make this mistake, be prepared to answer for why you still attend that church. Perhaps it was planted by a mega-church, or by an exciting new leader, which will make you seem like a pioneer. Perhaps it went through a recent "church split," which means the devil has been at work and you are working hard to regain lost ground. But if you have no good explanation for attending a church so small, you may be seen as staying in your "comfort zone" and not doing enough for the Lord. After all, mini-churches can't mount significant evangelism efforts or mission trips— unless they have a wealthy benefactor, and the only reason a wealthy benefactor stays with a mini-church is because he is getting a kick out of controlling the pastor. Rather than get into messy discussions of this sort, avoid saying you belong to a mini-church.

Avoid saying you belong to a mega-church. If you claim membership in a mega-church, be prepared to answer a lot of questions about the multiplied ministries of your church. You will be treated as an ambassador. Also, you run the risk that your conversation partner will know all the churches in your city and won't have heard of yours. The safest way to circumnavigate this is to introduce the number of people before you name the church:

QUESTIONER: Tell me about your church.

YOU: It's a church of two thousand just south of St. Louis.

QUESTIONER: Oh, you mean Christian Life Center?

YOU: That's the one.

QUESTIONER: I've heard of that church! My cousin goes there. Darlene Knobby.

YOU: Really. Maybe I'd recognize her.

QUESTIONER: I bet you would!

Mega-churches introduce too many thorny problems for the person faking evangelicalism. Instead, claim membership in a church of 500 to 1,500. This is the easiest way to sail past this question and avoid further scrutiny. Churches of this size are never well known outside their cities, and they are not expected to be inventive or groundbreaking. They are medium-sized and solid and have grown neither large enough to be interesting nor small enough to be embarrassing. That is the best kind for you to belong to.

DEEPER CONVERSATION

Once your church of origin has been established, and your commitment sussed out, your conversation partner may want to broach other topics, such as politics or newsworthy events. (If he asks for your testimony, don't try to fake it; just drop your Diet Coke and run.) The best way to steer

through these discussions is to assume the personality of the average Republican. Don't be aggressively conservative, but do agree with what everyone else is saying by nodding your head and saying, "Mm," as if touched deep in your spirit. If you are asked to express your opinion, say, "I agree with [name the person who spoke most recently and restate his or her position]."

TOPICS OF CONVERSATION

UNSAFE TOPICS

Madonna

Condoms

Quentin Tarantino movies

Hollywood

Bill or Hillary Clinton

Gays

MTV

The Supreme Court

What time the adult fare starts on HBO

SAFE TOPICS

Football

Ronald Reagan

Homeschooling

Michael W. Smith

Your latest Study Bible

During conversation you should season your responses with phrases like, "Praise God," "God is good," and, on occasion, "Praise Jesus." Evangelicals never say, "Praise the Father," or "Praise the Holy Spirit." Perhaps it's because those phrases don't sound spontaneous, or because they sound like one is trying to pick a fight about the Trinity. In any case, don't go overboard with phrases of agreement. Evangelicals have amazing noses for outsiders, and if you don't calibrate your level of "Christian-ese" to match theirs, they might realize you're shining them on.

JOKES

If the occasion calls for it, try out a few jokes, but follow these rules. Avoid anything of a sexual nature, as well as any joke that begins, "A guy walks into a bar. . . ." You'll lose your evangelical audience right there. Avoid racially insensitive jokes, blasphemous jokes, and jokes about homosexuals, just to be safe. Skip "pearly gates" jokes and jokes about religious leaders in airplanes with too few parachutes. This leaves knock-knock jokes. Here are some gems that will appeal to your evangelical audience:

> Knock-knock.
> *Who's there?*
> Pastor.
> *Pastor who?*
> Pastor potatoes, I'm hungry!
>
> Knock-knock.
> *Who's there?*
> Elder.

Elder who?

There'll be elder pay if you don't give your life to Jesus!

IF YOU ARE FOUND OUT

If you make a mistake that exposes you as an impostor, you may employ the conventional method of escape and bolt from the room, perhaps overturning tables and drink carts on the way out to deter anyone who wants to evangelize you. But if you want or need to maintain relationships with these evangelicals, the best strategy is to adopt an air of confusion and spiritual hunger. Granted, you will have to ward off many offers to receive Jesus. But you can unwind later with your favorite nonvirgin drink.

If you want to gain instant celebrity status in the room, claim to be a Jew who wants to learn more about Jesus. All socializing will stop, a hush will fall, and people will circle by to see you. Nothing excites evangelicals more than a Jew coming to Jesus. It is not only as rare as a liberal in Louisville, but it signals to them that the end times are near.

If you are unfortunate enough to look Arabic, just run.

WHAT TO SAY UPON DEPARTURE

Evangelicals turn in early, especially evangelical men on business trips, because they need at least two hours to struggle properly with their desire to masturbate. This is an important part of their schedule. When it's time to say good-bye, say:

"Blessings."

"God bless you."

"Have a blessed day/evening."

"Stay strong."

"I'll be praying for you."

"See you here, there, or in the air."

"Say hey to your pastor for me."

"This was a God appointment."

"I see the Lord in you."

"I'll take your words to heart."

"Say hi to those eight kids of yours."

SAMPLE EXCHANGE AND REACTER EXERCISE

A typical conversation between two seasoned evangelicals might go like this:

BOB: Hello, brother.

DAVE: Praise God, how are you?

BOB: Better than I was yesterday, but not as good as I'll be tomorrow.

DAVE: Amen. How's the family?

BOB: My daughter's on a short-term mission trip to Africa. God's doing awesome things in her life.

DAVE: Praise God. I'll keep her in prayer during my devotions this week.

BOB: I appreciate that. I've got to head into second service. Have a blessed week.

DAVE: You too, brother.

Now fill in the blanks of this conversation:

KATHY: Praise (1)_____(Buddha/God/Allah/myself)! I just heard my sister is having a baby.

DARLA: What a (2)_____ (crock/blessing/pain in the neck)! Children are a (3)_____ (nuisance/headache/heritage from the Lord). How's your week going?

KATHY: Fine, but I'm still recovering from that all-night (4)_____ (prayer meeting/bender/Viagra session).

DARLA: I'll be lifting you up in my (5)_____ (yoga class/prayer group/session with a medium). We should have your family over for (6)_____ (margaritas/fellowship/an Amway meeting).

KATHY: This must be (7)_____ (karma/a God thing/cosmic convergence). I was thinking the same thing! I was just reading in (8)_____ (*Glamour* magazine/Dr. Phil's latest book/First Peter) that hospitality is a key to good health.

DARLA: (9)_____ (Amen/Leave me alone/I'm done talking to you). By the way, did you hear? Season three of (10)_____ (*The Simpsons/The Sopranos/Touched by an Angel*) is out on DVD?

KATHY: I'll have to buy it. Gotta go. See you (11)_____ (here, there, or in the air/at the bar after work/down at Weight Watchers).

DARLA: (12)_____ (Screw/Bless) you.

ANSWERS:

1. God

2. blessing

3. heritage from the Lord

4. prayer meeting

5. prayer group

6. fellowship or Amway meeting

7. a God thing

8. First Peter

9. Amen

10. *Touched by an Angel*

11. here, there, or in the air

12. Bless

Chapter 6
HOW TO TALK
AND ACT LIKE
AN EVANGELICAL
WITHOUT BEING ONE

SIGHTING EVANGELICALS OVERSEAS

Responding to the Third World's incessant demand for white American proselytizers, evangelicals spend billions of dollars each year sending missionaries to the far corners of the world. These front-line evangelicals struggle with many challenges: How do I get clean water? Where should I dig my next pit latrine? How do I get Fox News out here in the jungle?

Though they have a reputation as culturally incurious bumpkins, the truth is that evangelicals crisscross the globe to inquire humbly of native peoples, "Will you accept Jesus, or do you want to burn in hell alongside your demon gods?" Thus, you can find evangelicals wherever you travel, and you might even bump into them on your next overseas vacation. This chapter will teach you how to identify the two kinds of evangelical missionary.

HOW MISSIONARIES BECOME MISSIONARIES

Through extensive study, evangelicals have concluded that the best-equipped people to carry the gospel to remote parts of the world are Caucasian midwesterners with strong regional accents. Evangelicals shrewdly understand that few people are better prepared to serve in, say, tribal Africa than someone born and raised in a Christian home in rural Nebraska.

As young people, evangelicals are encouraged to become missionaries because their parents would rather they ended up in Belize teaching "This Little Light of Mine" to tribespeople than at Harvard taking Jell-O shots and sleeping with their TA. To evangelicals, the mission field is the Ivy League, which is why so many high school grads in Des Moines grasp for greatness by entering missionary service. It also gives many of them a meaningful alternative to temping.

Long-term missionaries are those who spend a lifetime in the mission field. The decision to become a long-term missionary is usually made soberly and thoughtfully while blubbering at the church altar with twenty other impressionable teenagers after a browbeater of a sermon. This is the evangelical version of career counseling. Missionary candidates then enroll in language school long enough to learn key phrases like "Trust Jesus" and "Where's the nearest ice cream shop?" When they arrive in the mission field, they are welcomed by local people eager to hear twenty-four-year-old graduates of Grand Forks Bible College rail against their ancient spiritual traditions.

Once in the mission field, missionaries set about converting native peoples and raising socially maladjusted children known as MKs, which stands for "missionary kids" and for "much kounseling," which they will need after growing up in New Guinea and returning to the United States for college. Missionaries also busy themselves hosting groups of visiting American evangelicals there for sightseeing trips and personal spiritual transformation. These are called "short-term missionaries," and they will be discussed in due course.

Smart missionaries know that ample girth demonstrates the blessing of the Lord and helps distinguish them from Peace Corps volunteers. This is why they budget several hundred dollars a year to ship in foods like peanut

THE FIVE STAGES OF A MISSIONARY'S LIFE

STAGE 1: ELATION—"I've been called by God."

STAGE 2: REALITY—"Uganda is nothing like Wichita."

STAGE 3: ACCULTURATION—"Honey, get away from that wildebeest corpse!"

STAGE 4: BREAKDOWN—"My life is ruined. I want to go home and work for Dad's insurance business."

STAGE 5: ACCEPTANCE—"Honey, drag that wildebeest corpse over here and let's have dinner."

MISSIONARY KIDS SUE PARENTS FOR "SUCKY, NON-WESTERN UPBRINGING"

ORLANDO, FLA.—Children of missionaries have filed a class-action lawsuit against their parents for raising them in "disgusting, disease-ridden parts of the world" like Indonesia, Cambodia, and virtually anywhere in Africa.

"It's about time we took our destiny into our own hands," says Marsha Limnell, 22, an MK who now lives in Pittsburgh, Pa., and who went through five years of trauma counseling after growing up in Uganda. "I mean, who would ask to be raised in Kampala?"

The children say they have a "right to be raised in conditions equivalent to those in the country of their citizenship." In effect, it means that raising a U.S. citizen in substandard conditions elsewhere in the world could be considered child abuse.

Cameron Leftengle, 17, grew up in Malaysia and was convinced she was leading the kind of life most other kids would envy, until she returned to Illinois as a second-grader and ran into a spate of cultural transition issues.

"I remember squatting on the playground and defecating during recess, like we did in Malaysia," she says. "The kids laughed at me, and I got sent to the principal's office. I was humiliated."

She was also embarrassed when her classmates found she'd brought toasted crickets and fire ants for lunch.

"The scars from those experiences are hard to overcome," she says. "My life was basically ruined."

From LarkNews.com, a good source of Christian news

butter and Ritz crackers to help maintain their heft in countries with few reliable sources of saturated fats.

HOW MISSIONARIES MAKE A LIVING

Long-term missionaries spend every third year traveling the United States and regaling smitten evangelical audiences with stories of miracles, angelic visitations, and encounters with demon-possessed witch doctors. As the main supplier of adventure tales and urban legends in the evangelical universe, they are obliged to relate more fantastic experiences with each visit. They also dress in the perceived traditional clothing from their country of service, playing to Americans' mistaken belief that Third World residents dress in colorful handcrafted garb. In fact, most Third World residents wear used American clothing that was shipped there because it wouldn't sell for a nickel at a garage sale in Grand Rapids anymore. But missionaries know that if they showed up to preach in an old *NSync T-shirt and ill-fitting swim trunks, nobody would give them a dime.

To tug the heartstrings, missionaries show videos of poor children until the audience is overwhelmed by guilt. Then the church takes up an offering so the missionary can live in the mission field for two more years. This entire process is called itinerating, and it ensures that missionaries don't have to get real jobs in their country of service.

If you get the chance to hear a missionary raise money at an evangelical church, use this "Missionary Decoder" tool to understand what he is saying:

When the missionary says . . .	The missionary means . . .
"We had a great revival."	I preached.
"The whole village came out."	All twelve of them.
"There was a powerful move of God."	Nobody fell asleep during the sermon.
"Half the people were saved."	Six kids raised their hands.
"People were healed."	An old man said his back felt better.
"One young lady saw angels on the platform beside me."	My skin was so white, some people were seeing double.
"Demons were cast out of people."	That screaming baby finally fell asleep.
"Revival spread throughout that entire region."	After a while, people went home.
"Please give generously so more people can be saved."	I'd really like to keep doing this.

THE SIGHTING EXCURSION

While drinking cheap mai tais by the resort pool on your next overseas vacation, you may get the itch to sight evangelicals. But it can be tricky distinguishing between missionaries and UN workers, especially if it's only 6:00 P.M. and the UN workers are not yet drunk and hitting on the local women.

Here are some hints: Evangelical missionaries don't have that nihilistic air most aid workers get after years of dispiriting service, and they don't read *Le Monde* international edition like retired diplomats. Unlike dull-eyed

TEEN SEEKS MISSION ASSIGNMENT WHERE WOMEN DON'T WEAR CLOTHES

INDIANAPOLIS, IND.—Billy Pratt, 17, of Shafter Community Church, is seeking a short-term mission trip to any locale where women hang around naked.

"There are places in the world where people just don't wear clothes," he says, perched on his bed at his parents' house. Pratt has researched locations extensively on the Internet. He says that if teen boys could work in a place where they were surrounded by "tons and tons of boobs," the ranks of missionaries would swell.

"I don't know why they don't publish this stuff," he says.

Pratt hopes his church will send him on an exploratory trip to remote Brazil and perhaps the French Riviera—"wherever unclothed people need to hear the gospel," he says. He is collecting Bibles to give away and has 100 memory cards for his digital camera. He expects to garner financial support from teenage boys who, in exchange for their donation, will receive the password to Pratt's website, which will include video updates and a slide show of his mission work.

He hopes his church sees the urgency of sending him.

"I have a meeting with the pastor next week," he says. "We'll see how it goes."

From LarkNews.com, a good source of Christian news

Chapter 7
SIGHTING
EVANGELICALS
OVERSEAS

ex-pats, they don't have subservient local wives, and they don't walk with a spring in their step like American businessmen setting up new child-labor factories. Unlike Peace Corps volunteers, they can't be found speaking blissfully about Third World debt cancellation or enjoying late-night sex in their tents.

Rather, look for happy Americans sitting in cafés near embassy row, reading the latest million-selling devotional book and enjoying the fact that nobody from the United States knows they're taking the month off from evangelizing the natives.

Most importantly, short-term mission trips allow evangelicals to alleviate world hunger and poverty through the ministries of clowning, puppetry, and mime.

STAGES OF A SHORT-TERM MISSION TRIP

1. EXCITEMENT—"I'm leaving Kentucky/West Virginia/South Carolina for the first time!"

2. SHOCK UPON ARRIVAL—"Look at this poverty."

3. ATTACHMENT TO LOCAL CHILD—"God knit our hearts."

4. TEARFUL DEPARTURE—"Maybe I'm supposed to be a missionary here."

5. RIGHTEOUS ANGER AT U.S. CHURCH—"We're backslidden compared to those Ecuadorean Christians."

6. EVENTUAL RETURN TO TORPOR—"Pass the Doritos."

FANTASY CAMP FOR SHORT-TERM MISSIONARIES

America's abundant wealth has put the world within reach of even the most sheltered Christian families, who can experience the thrills and diseases of the mission field just as readily as middle-aged men enjoy a week at fantasy baseball camp. These people are called short-term missionaries, which is defined as any evangelical who spends thousands of dollars and a week of vacation time to help a long-term missionary do a task, like church construction, that could have been done for pennies if the money had been used to hire locals.

Short-term mission trips give average evangelicals the feeling of doing something valuable for the Kingdom and assuage their lingering guilt over their latest SUV purchase. It also gives them a rare opportunity to see Mexicans in a context other than fieldwork or bussing tables.

But most important, short-term mission trips allow evangelicals to alleviate world hunger and poverty through the ministries of clowning, puppetry, and mime. Rather than participate in feeding or literacy programs, which offer only a fleeting solution, evangelicals go to the root of the Third World's problems: lack of sufficient open-air entertainment.

While sightseeing in the plaza of a foreign city, you may spy a knot of young thespians with faces painted black and white, performing a drama to music. Is it a wayward group of G-8 convention protesters? A therapy exercise for agoraphobics? A promotion for an upcoming Marcel Marceau performance?

SPRING BREAK PARTYING IN CANCÚN VERSUS SPRING BREAK ON SHORT-TERM MISSION TRIP

	SHORT-TERM MISSION	CANCÚN
PURPOSE OF TRIP	Engage in missionary work and bond with local people	Engage in "missionary" work and bond with local people
NECESSARY ACCESSORY	40-oz. bottle of Purell	40-oz. bottle of Jose Cuervo tequila
SLEEPING ARRANGEMENT	12 people on the floor of a half-built church	12 people in a room at the Beachcomber Motel
MAJOR SIDE BENEFIT	Church bragging rights	Frat house bragging rights
POSSIBLE SIDE EFFECTS	Montezuma's revenge, malaria	Monster hangover, VD

HELPFUL HEADLINE

CHURCH SENDS CLOWN AND PUPPET TEAMS TO WAR-TORN AFRICA

KENEMA, SIERRA LEONE—Short-term mission teams from South Coast Community Church in New Orleans, La., arrived in this country racked by three decades of civil war and began serving the ravaged people through the ministries of clowning and puppetry.

"I'm so excited about this trip, I've been practicing my puppet moves for months," said Linda Chapin, 45, as she made mouthing movements with her fingers.

The teams' first performances were in Makeni, a city in the north where one-third of the population has been brutally slaughtered in factional fighting, and those people who remain have no reliable source of food or water. Thousands of children, many with grotesque potbellies and limbs cut off by machete-wielding rebels, gathered around the makeshift stage to watch the South Coast teams perform funny skits.

"This war has been terrible," said one local mother of six who'd lost her husband to rebel violence three months earlier. "We've been hoping somebody would take notice of our plight and send us clowns and puppets."

Later, in a refugee camp outside Kenema, the teams set up their puppet stage, handmade from PVC pipes and blue cloth. As Sierra Leoneans gathered, clowns entertained them, squirting silly string on each other and shaping balloons into wiener dogs and setting them on the children's heads.

"I haven't eaten for three days," said François, 7, one of the lucky ones to get a balloon, "but when I see the clowns and puppets, I get a good feeling inside."

Some children and adults put pages from the gospel tracts into their mouths, hoping the ink would make them high.

The South Coast clown and puppet teams returned to New Orleans and reported to the church about their powerful ministry in Sierra Leone.

"When you see the looks on those kids' faces, you realize why you went," said one clown and puppet team member before breaking down.

Owing to the ministry of the clown and puppet teams, 246 children had made decisions for Christ and 119 made recommitments. The church intends to send expanded clown and puppet teams next year.

From LarkNews.com, a good source of Christian news

The message evangelicals hope to send to local observers is that Jesus cares for them so much that he sent a dozen Iowan teenagers to perform mime skits they wrote themselves.

BUILDING YOUR DREAM HOME WITH EVANGELICALS' HELP

If you would like to build a dream vacation home overseas, and you would like evangelicals to pay for it, follow these steps:

1. Convince a U.S. church you are a missionary. Send out photocopied, badly folded newsletters telling about your overseas "work." Fill the newsletter with photographs of local Hispanic children you hired to play in a muddy vacant lot wearing only their underwear. Make up testimonies about how their parents met Jesus through your efforts.

2. Head to your country of choice and start scheduling short-term mission trips. Hire fifty locals to play the part of your church congregation.

3. Host a team from the United States to build the "church sanctuary" (i.e., your house). Deposit their cash donation in an offshore bank in the Bahamas.

3. Take the team sightseeing and trinket shopping.

4. Break into tears of gratitude as you say good-bye at the airport.

5. Keep sending out newsletters and scheduling teams as needed to finish your estate.

No, it's American evangelical teenagers communicating the gospel in the international language of street drama. Take a moment to watch and the theme of good and evil will unfold as angels and demons battle over a particular person's soul, climaxing when Jesus, played by the tallest and handsomest boy in the youth group, embraces the beleaguered sinner. The message evangelicals hope to send to local observers is that Jesus cares for them so much that he sent a dozen Iowan teenagers to perform mime skits they wrote themselves.

Puppetry and clowning are the other main tools of the short-term missionary. Head to foreign slums and you will see American evangelicals dressed up as clowns and handing out gospel literature. You will also see Bible-themed puppet shows. You will know they are evangelical puppet shows, and not some experimental UN program, because at the end you will experience the delightfully surreal moment when a puppet leads the crowd in the sinner's prayer.

Spotting short-term missionaries is easy once you know what to look for. Failing all else, watch for Americans wearing WWJD bracelets and vomiting up the local cuisine.

Having learned to sight evangelicals anywhere in the world, let's bring the evangelical experience back home—and into your living room.

Chapter 7
SIGHTING
EVANGELICALS
OVERSEAS

NICE THINGS MISSIONARIES SAY WHEN LEAVING THE MISSION FIELD FOR GOOD

"Nothing against Namibia, but we're ready for a change of pace."

"No, you may not come with me in my luggage."

"Of course you may visit. My new address is 1600 Pennsylvania Avenue, Washington, D.C."

"God did tell us to come here. And last night as I was puking out my other kidney, I distinctly heard him say I should go back to Nebraska."

Chapter 8

DECORATING LIKE AN EVANGELICAL

Few abodes match the comfort and conservatism of those decorated by evangelicals. Instead of keeping up with endless turns of the fashion wheel, evangelicals embrace a long-term design scheme that conveys stability, simplicity, and moral clarity. That's why, in some cutting-edge quarters of Paris and New York, decorating like an evangelical has become the latest craze, sending fashionistas flocking to Bible bookstores for Kinkade paintings, Precious Moments figurines, and other evangelical accoutrements with which to adorn their Montmartre flats and Upper West Side apartments. Clearly, after fussing with assembly-required IKEA furniture and nondescript contemporary offerings from Pottery Barn and Pier 1, the world now yearns for that distinctly evangelical sensibility.

This chapter offers a detailed guide to the finer points of evangelical home decorating for the ambitious homeowner who wishes to infuse his or her living space with that particular *je ne sais quoi* that says, "Evangelicals live here."

THE ENTRYWAY

The first set of uniquely evangelical touches should appear as you approach the front door. There hang a wooden tole-painted angel wearing a silly grin and bearing a banner that reads, BLESS THIS HOME! Add wind chimes with a wind-catcher bearing a Christian sentiment such as, AND HIS ENTIRE HOUSEHOLD WAS SAVED. ACTS 9. Similar thoughts or blessings may be stenciled onto rocks and set among the plants.

There is no need to buy a special doormat, as this would be an inappropriate place to put scripture verses. A simple mat that reads WELCOME! or WELCOME, FRIENDS! will do.

On the wall immediately visible when you walk in, hang a framed cross-stitch or embroidery that reads, AS FOR ME AND MY HOUSE, WE WILL SERVE THE LORD. JOSHUA 3. There is simply no substitute for this particular piece if you wish to maintain a convincing evangelical design. It declares to friends and visitors alike that the home is fully under Jesus's control, and nothing can be done about it. Evangelicals can be reasonable and accepting in the public sphere, but when it comes to their own homes, they see no reason to be subtle about their allegiances. As an added bonus, this particular statement conveys a sense of guilt to wayward teenage children who break curfew and slink home after partying all night.

As a rule, cross-stitches and embroideries should be hung liberally throughout the home to remind people that LOVE IS PATIENT, LOVE IS KIND or that they can DO ALL THINGS THROUGH CHRIST WHO STRENGTHENS ME. Cross-stitch and embroidery replete with butterflies and flowers are among the most enduring pillars of evangelical decor. Inexpensive samples can be picked up at secondhand stores and garage sales.

THE LIVING ROOM

The focal point of your living room should be a massive painting by Thomas Kinkade with an elaborate wooden frame and a small brass plaque bearing the painting's title. The painting should be at least as large as a child's swimming pool, and lit with track lighting. Kinkade, an evangelical himself, imbues his paintings with religious themes and the moral clarity that is the backbone of this design scheme. Evangelical families spend thousands on original Kinkade paintings and show them off with the same pride with which SoHo residents show off the Warhol pencil sketch they bought off a down-on-their-luck artist friend.

Apart from Kinkade paintings, there should be no "real" art in the home, especially paintings or sculptures. Evangelicals eschew modern art, which strikes them as superfluous, sensual, and deviant—the fatalistic soul-language of liberal New Yorkers and the dissipated rich. Sculpture, especially, is almost never seen in the evangelical home, except for molds of praying hands picked up at the Bible bookstore.

Now to the living room furniture, which should be cushioned and comfortable, in the style of a midpriced

CHRISTIAN CRIBS
See How the Other Saints Live

MTV
MUSIC TELEVISION®

CHECK LOCAL LISTINGS

Chapter 8
DECORATING LIKE
AN EVANGELICAL

hotel lobby. Don't veer in the direction of Scandinavian minimalism, as it would speak of European godlessness. Rather, obtain an overstuffed couch with a floral print and cozy throw pillows to provide purple and peach chromatic counterpoint. Add hardwood end tables with glass tops, the kind of solid, amysterious furniture you can get at Sears. (A major advantage of the evangelical decorating scheme is that it can be done on a tight budget, especially if a local dentist's office or Motel 6 is going out of business.) Matching lamps with pleated accordion shades will give off decisive but not glaring light. On the back of the couch place a throw blanket with a portrait of Jesus carrying a lamb slung around his shoulders. The walls should be painted an agreeable cream color, or you may venture gingerly into pastels. There should be no hard reds or blacks to jar the thoughts.

Enliven the rest of the living room with smaller details—on the mantel, porcelain and crystal angels, their robes flowing in an unseen heavenly breeze. On the coffee table, handmade lace doilies, recalling a previous era of shared values. There too put a *Prayer of Jabez* personal journal, the last three issues of *Decision* magazine, and the latest Left Behind novel, distressed to appear much-read.

On the secondary wall, counterbalancing the Kinkade, hang a large portrait of your family. Dad, Mom, and kids should be dressed in tan slacks and dresses, and leaning against a large oak tree in a park. The portrait's edges should be airbrushed, adding an ethereal quality. (Why the family is hanging around the park in such nice clothes need not be answered. The point is that wherever they find themselves, they are neat, pressed, and delighted to be together.)

The father should be the focal point of the portrait, embodying virility and paternal devotion in perfect equilibrium. The mother should present a strong subtheme of feminine strength and support; the bright-faced children should be arrayed around them like piles of treasure.

If you lack the family members to make such a portrait, hire friends to play the various roles of father, mother, and children. Or ask an evangelical family if you can have a copy of their portrait and then have yourself airbrushed in among them.

Note: In the evangelical home you will *not* see the kind of portraiture that has recently come into fashion: semi-nude mothers cuddling their naked babies, draped in white linen. In the evangelical family portrait, there is no hint of sensuality or passion but rather uprightness and the promise of generations of fruitful monogamy.

THE KITCHEN

In the kitchen, cultivate a feeling of friendly disarray. The entire home should be permeated by the smell of a warm casserole baking in the oven. The refrigerator should be a kaleidoscope of newspaper clippings, family photographs, and columns by James Dobson. Hang the latest photograph and letter from the Honduran child "your" family is supporting with a monthly contribution of $25. Post last week's sermon notes and Sunday school drawings and a magnet that says, EXPECT A MIRACLE! Procure a "missionary magnet" that depicts a happy family from rural Wisconsin now serving in Ethiopia. The magnet will request prayer and financial support. To round out the informal collage, write up a chore list, post a

prayer list, and display a large photo of the most recent Republican president.

Remove all alcohol-related paraphernalia, including wall hangings that incorporate wine or beer into the artistic theme. Turn that built-in wine rack into a handy sock-holder for the time being.

Then go for the finer touches. Above the sink hang a leaded-glass sun-catcher that depicts a cross on a hillside. Throw in a Thomas Kinkade calendar where you can, and post a silly little sign that reads, BLESS THIS MESS! Replace the functional light-switch plate with a ceramic lighthouse, its golden beam shining outward. Near the doorway, post a dry erase board and jot down appointments that would fit an evangelical family schedule: a women's ministry meeting, a men's breakfast, youth choir practice. Draw a smiley face in the corner and scribble, "This is the day the LORD has made! I will REJOICE and be glad in it!"

THE FAMILY ROOM

The entertainment room of the house should include a media cabinet crammed with Gaithers' Homecoming DVDs and every VeggieTales video ever made. The radio or CD player should offer constant worship music in the background, to calm the atmosphere and train the mind on godly things during idle moments. The worship music should, of course, be Christian; no tribal drumming or Indian sitars.

Against the wall, place a simple brown spinet with a hymnal open to "Amazing Grace." The piano keys should be chipped and worn from years of service during piano lessons and family worship times. Set up a china hutch to

Remove all alcohol-related paraphernalia. Turn that built-in wine rack into a handy sock-holder for the time being.

display a collection of sad-eyed Precious Moments figurines, a ceramic Kinkade village, and antique dishware that appears to have been passed down from godly Christian forebears.

DAD'S OFFICE

Convert one of your rooms to "Dad's office," which should smell of cherrywood, because of Dad's new desk suite, with an underlying note of leather from his black swivel chair. On the desk place several ceramic eagles in flight, a glass golf ball paperweight, a 365-day golf jokes calendar, and a notepad with a Bible verse preprinted at the top of each sheet. On the corner set a men's devotional book—the kind he might be studying with his Thursday morning accountability group.

Surround the desk with dozens of family photos, which help "Dad" keep his universe correctly aligned while at work. Include a large department store portrait that shows "Dad" and "Mom" sitting one-two, like stair steps, smiling and still in love after twenty-eight years. Next to it put a smaller photo of him on a recent mission trip to the Dominican Republic.

Complete the office ensemble with an oil painting of an eagle and the words of Isaiah 40, "They that wait upon the Lord will renew their strength; they will mount up with wings as eagles," written in script. Hang another painting of the Founding Fathers at prayer. On a bookshelf put the complete hardbound set of Left Behind books in order of publication. For complete authenticity, the first one should be autographed by Jerry Jenkins and Tim LaHaye.

If you are decorating for an evangelical teenage boy, give the appearance of independence and rebellion while not actually promoting sex, rock music, or the black-death fixation some high schoolers fall into.

MOM'S SEWING ROOM

This room ideally would sit adjacent to the laundry room. It is your repository of domestic crafts and should smell of fabric and scented candles. Stenciled doves and flowers on the walls will tie the room together. Drape the Hide-a-Bed couch (the room doubles as a guest bedroom for relatives or visiting missionaries) with half-completed quilts and a Sunday dress that needs hem repair. On the nightstand, put an imposing row of Janette Oke historical romance novels and a cross-stitch that states simply, FAITH, HOPE, AND LOVE. In the wall outlet nearest the door put a nightlight of praying hands.

THE GUEST BATHROOM

Evangelicals see their guest bathrooms as opportunities to convert unsaved visitors. Fill yours with spiritual reminders—a mounted sand dollar with the story of the starfish legend etched into it and a glazed wood piece that bears the prose offering "Footsteps in the Sand" (see appendices for complete texts). On the back of the toilet have a dog-eared copy of My *Utmost for His Highest,* an extra roll of toilet paper in a crocheted yarn slipcover, a whimsical set of church-mouse candleholders, and a candid photo of the family at the Sea of Galilee during a recent tour of the Holy Land.

Next to the medicine cabinet hang a plaque that reads, GOD, GRANT ME THE SERENITY TO ACCEPT THE THINGS I CANNOT CHANGE, THE COURAGE TO CHANGE THE THINGS I CAN, AND THE WISDOM TO KNOW THE DIFFERENCE. In the cabinet there should be nothing more scandalous than an old container of Sea Breeze and a tube of Clearasil.

THE KIDS' BEDROOMS

In the bedroom wing, affix a plaque to the door of each child's bedroom that gives the biblical definition of that child's name (BRIANNA: STRENGTH. SHE WILL BE STRONG FOR THE KINGDOM OF GOD). In the hallway hang as many photographs of the family as the wall studs can reasonably handle.

Commission a mural of Noah's Ark for a young child's bedroom, with animals and the ark situated on rolling green hills, a rainbow arcing overhead, and eight happy people wearing simple robes and headbands. If that is beyond your budget, pink paint will do for girls, and blue for boys. Over the daybed place a painting of Jesus watching over a sleeping child. For younger children, line the walls with VeggieTales plush toys.

If you are decorating for an evangelical teenage boy, give the appearance of independence and rebellion while not actually promoting sex, rock music, or the black-death fixation some high schoolers fall into. This is accomplished with "edgy" snowboard, skateboard, and/or BMX posters and posters from scruffy-looking Christian rock bands. Lay an Adventure Bible open on the bed, and slip a year's worth of *Campus Life* magazines under the bed.

A teenage girl's room will look much the same, but with posters of Michael W. Smith. On the dresser, place a small white New Testament next to a Promise ring nestled in a jewelry box. Include a book or two about the Proverbs 31 woman, to prep her for a lifetime of women's ministry events. Avoid magazines like *Seventeen* and *CosmoGirl!*, which encourage teen sex and public belly button display.

Chapter 8
DECORATING LIKE
AN EVANGELICAL

THE MASTER BEDROOM

The master bedroom should be engulfed in sumptuous quasi-southern luxury. Go to Kmart for floral-print bedding and a bedskirt. Adorn the bed with an avalanche of pillows, drapes at the head, and a faux-antique settee at its foot. In the corner of the room, place a table-and-chair ensemble, with Mom's personal prayer journal and Study Bible and a coaster for her coffee mug. A rack of *Today's Christian Woman* magazines and the latest novel in the Mitford series should be within easy reach.

In the master bathroom, place framed scriptures and groupings of flowers and candles suitable for extended baths and "special times" with the Lord. The masculine influence will be slight in the master bathroom. After all, "Dad" would rather be in his office.

And so, with a surfeit of inspirational ornaments and a small financial investment, you can deck your home in one of the most up-to-date fashion schemes. Not only that, but your most committed evangelical friends will feel right at home, and you too will enjoy the cheer, surety, and simplicity of this classic American design.

Chapter 9

EVANGELICAL MATING HABITS

Most people associate the words "evangelical sex" with words like "boring," "traditional," and "televangelist." But the fact is, if you are not having highly satisfying sex four times a week, it's probably because you are not an evangelical. Over the past thirty years, surveys show that evangelicals have sex more often, and find it more satisfying, than any other group—including urban single women and their various partners. While you are lying in bed wondering if your boyfriend really loves you, married evangelical couples are achieving orgasm almost nightly and then sleeping like babies.

It may not seem fair. How did America's Most Repressed become America's Most Sexually Satisfied? Or is it all a ruse to convert people to heterosexual monogamy?

This chapter explores the strange and wonderful habits of evangelical sex and explodes the myth that they are anything but tigers in the bedroom. It also offers between-the-sheets advice from the Bible itself.

RAISING VIRGINS IN TROUBLED TIMES

Next to salvation, nothing matters more to evangelicals than their virginity, which they preserve with the vigilance of guards at Fort Knox. "Sex is for when you say, 'I do,' and heavy petting belongs at the zoo," goes the saying. If you have sex before marriage—and statistics indicate you probably have—it is called "fornication" or "hiding in the balcony with the pastor's son." Every good evangelical knows that God has a much more difficult time forgiving sexual impurity than he does sins like gossip, judgmentalism, and neglecting the poor.

To promote virginity, evangelicals pour a great deal of energy into abstinence education, which perpetuates healthy ignorance of condoms. Fanatical virgins even attend abstinence rallies and sign abstinence pledges. Some wear a Promise ring or small gold key that symbolizes, in beautiful fetish form, their commitment to refrain from sex until they are seventeen and can legally marry. Waiting not only spares them the attention of the high school football team but delivers terrific laughs on their wedding night when two pimply virgins fumble through their first shot at procreation without the benefit of liquor, previous experience, or postcoital cigarettes. And for ugly adolescents who couldn't find a sex partner if they tried,

CHRISTIAN COUPLE MAINTAINS ABSTINENCE THROUGH FIRST TWO YEARS OF MARRIAGE

TOPEKA, KAN.—Jon and Darla Nusbaum, who dutifully abstained from sex during their fourteen-month courtship, have remained abstinent after marriage and plan to do so indefinitely.

"If it was holy before, it must be double-holy afterwards," Darla says.

Having now completed twenty-five months of marriage without any sexual contact, they go about their normal lives, jobs, and social calendar with no hint of relational strain.

Sometimes after dinner they will kiss in the kitchen and "start having bedroom thoughts," Darla says, but they never fail to pull back. Darla breaks away to spray cool, misted water on her face. Jon eats a whole raw potato to take himself out of the mood.

They don't know when they'll finally break the pledge, and they feel no pressure. After abstaining so long before marriage, "a few extra years is nothing," says Darla.

"Of course, we don't lord it over any other couple who decides to have sex after marriage, but for us it's about staying faithful to the abstinence message and the holiness involved with that," says Jon, who seems unbothered. "For us, true love waits, and waits, and waits."

From LarkNews.com, a good source of Christian news

the abstinence movement's I'M WORTH THE WAIT! lapel pin is a face-saving device.

Some evangelical girls go further and actually "date Jesus," meaning they devote the time they would have spent dating to praying and communing with Christ. This has major benefits. Jesus never pressures them to have sex. He doesn't carry a lot of emotional baggage. But he also never pays for the date, and he's difficult to take to the prom. When a young woman decides to break up with Jesus and start dating actual humans, she is often disappointed.

SANCTIFIED SEX

All discussions about married evangelical sex must start, naturally, with Tim LaHaye. Long before LaHaye created the tense prose and complex characters that have made the Left Behind series so popular with discerning Kansas housewives, he wrote an explicit sex manual with his wife, and presumed sex partner, Beverly. The book, called *The Act of Marriage*, was published in 1976 and was meant to address the lack of decent sex being experienced by just-married eighteen-year-olds. The LaHayes, who are registered sex therapists in addition to being ready for the Rapture, offer frank advice of the *Joy of Sex* variety.

Warning: Readers under eighteen or with weak constitutions should stop reading here, as we are about to sample some advice from the most-read evangelical sex book of modern time.

The LaHayes, who are registered sex therapists in addition to being ready for the Rapture, offer frank advice of the *Joy of Sex* variety.

Excerpt #1

On first arousal the husband will be able to feel the clitoris with his fingers.... [His wife] may want him to insert one finger very gently into the vagina, making slow rhythmic movements inside while his other fingers continue contact with the outer vulval area. This will usually give her a delightful sensation and help to increase her excitement.

> —Tim and Beverly LaHaye,
> *The Act of Marriage*, pp. 102, 108

Excerpt #2

[The wife] should ... let herself go completely, so that if she wishes to groan, cry, wiggle, rotate, or thrust, she may do so.

> —Tim and Beverly LaHaye,
> *The Act of Marriage*, p. 108

Excerpt #3

[She] will go through several physiological changes as her excitement mounts. Her heart will palpitate, her skin becomes warm, and almost every part of her body becomes sensitive to the touch. Her breathing will be more rapid, her face may grimace as if in

pain, and she may groan audibly—and her husband finds this all very exhilarating.

—Tim and Beverly LaHaye,
The Act of Marriage, p. 102

If evangelicals take the advice given in *The Act of Marriage*—and there's every reason to believe they do, since the book has sold 2.5 million copies—they are enjoying sex lives the editors of *Glamour* magazine can only dream about. And with *The Act of Marriage* and *Left Behind* on their nightstands, evangelicals know that if the Lord returns while they are having sex, the LaHayes have them covered on both ends.

HOW EVANGELICALS TALK DIRTY

Evangelicals know another secret most people miss: the Bible is full of sexual how-tos. Who needs *Cosmopolitan*'s "10 Tips to Drive Your Man Wild" when the Old Testament offers bedroom advice that would make your mother blush? Who needs romance novels when Jacob, Leah, and Rachel are in a dramatic ménage à trois, with God taking sides from one episode to another?

The wisest man who ever lived, Solomon, wrote three books of the Bible, and one is a script for erotic dialogue. In the Song of Solomon (which, thanks to Tipper Gore, now carries a parental advisory label), two naked lovers explore the sights and smells of each other's intimate parts, driving themselves to delirious desire with still-fashionable compliments like,

> Your navel is a rounded goblet that never
> lacks blended wine. (Song of Solomon 7:2)

Or this:

> Your breasts [are] like clusters of fruit ... I
> will take hold of its fruit. (Song of Solomon 7:7)

And that's just the foreplay. As things get rolling, Solomon offers hot exchanges like these:

> HIM: Open to me, my sister, my darling, my dove,
> my flawless one. My head is drenched with dew,
> my hair with the dampness of night.

> HER: I have taken off my robe—must I put it on
> again?... My lover thrust his hand through the
> latch-opening; my heart began to pound for
> him. I arose to open for my lover, and my hands
> dripped with myrrh, my fingers flowing myrrh,
> on the handles of the lock. I opened for my lover.
> (Song of Solomon 5:2–5)

Solomon's sex tome was the standard for evangelical bedroom advice until the LaHayes plunged into the market 3,000 years later. But Solomon had one advantage over both of the LaHayes: with 700 wives and 300 mistresses, he was able to conduct wide-ranging sex surveys all by himself.

GOD AND SEX

Solomon's writings make it clear to evangelicals that God approves of hot sex. After all, it was God's idea for people

to walk around naked in the garden of Eden. When Adam and Eve sinned the result was . . . clothing, which marked the beginning of the fashion industry and the inevitable rise of *Vogue* magazine.

It's unclear what God thinks of other kinds of sex. He often disapproved of homosexuality but for a while didn't mind multiple wives or divorce. He also put prostitutes and adulterers in the messianic line and was not above using sexually charged insults like,

> **Therefore, whore, listen to God's message.**
>
> —Ezekiel 16:35

Or,

> **She lusted after her lovers, whose genitals were like those of donkeys and whose emission was like that of horses.**
>
> —Ezekiel 23:20

And then,

> **I will pull up your skirts over your face that your shame may be seen.**
>
> —Jeremiah 13:26

Clearly, sex is fair game in service of a well-placed put-down. But on a practical level, evangelicals know that the Bible offers much advice on common sexual quandaries faced by evangelicals and non-evangelicals alike.

For example, if your dad gets drunk and lies around the house naked (Genesis 9:21), or your boyfriend is a peeping tom (Song of Solomon 2:9), the Bible tells you what to do.

Maybe you want sex immediately, but can't find your mate (Song of Songs 3:1–5), or you need to sneak out of your boyfriend's apartment after spending the night with him (Ruth 3:14).

Perhaps you have grown bored with your wife's breasts (Proverbs 5:19–23), or you don't like your girlfriend's new tan (Song of Solomon 1:5–6). Does your husband stubbornly use the withdrawal method to avoid pregnancy (Genesis 38:9)? Has your wife, who can't get pregnant, asked you to sleep with the housekeeper (Genesis 16)? Consult the Good Book.

Some readers may want to have sex with a hooker but don't have cash on hand to pay for it (Genesis 38:17). Or perhaps a hooker has helped you out of a life-threatening situation (Joshua 2), or your wife has sold herself to a pimp (Hosea 3).

Say your boss's wife drags you to bed (Genesis 39:11–12), or the neighbor seduces you when her husband is on a business trip (Proverbs 7:19–27).

Or perhaps you are dying and your employees send a beautiful virgin to climb in bed with you to cheer you up. What should you do? (see I Kings 1:1–4).

Sexually adventurous readers might wonder how to respond if their girlfriend ties them up with ropes while they are sleeping (Judges 16:8) or when a gay orgy gets out of hand (Genesis 19). Perhaps you have gotten sexual fluids on your favorite leather shoes or handbag (Leviticus 15:17). Or, in extreme cases, you are fornicating and a man rushes into the room with a sword (Numbers 25).

Finally, Arkansans will find useful advice when they have gotten their daughter-in-law pregnant (Genesis 38), or when, on the morning after your wedding, the woman

you find in your bed is your bride's sister—and your father-in-law planned it that way (Genesis 29).

With the advice found in the Bible and *The Act of Marriage*, it shouldn't surprise anyone that evangelicals have wild sex lives most people know nothing about. The next time you spot a tired-looking evangelical mom in the grocery store, remember she was probably up all night—and it wasn't with the kids.

EVANGELICAL EDUCATION

More than just an oxymoron, "evangelical education" is a way of life for millions of Americans. The purpose of evangelical education, like the purpose of Fox News, is to dispense with contradictory ideas with as little thought as possible, resulting in eighteen-year-old biblically literate virgins who vote Republican.

THE HOMESCHOOL REVOLUTION

Evangelical education begins with homeschool, where Mom and Dad put on their "expert instructor" caps, set up a chalkboard in the living room, and teach tender minds that the Earth is 6,000 years old and Ollie North is an exemplary American. In the fiery kiln of the homeschool social experience, children are challenged to become fair-minded and tolerant of the wide spectrum of views held by other family members.

Free from hours of wasted interaction with heaven-impaired children, homeschoolers believe they receive a superior education. Parents cite other reasons as well for shunning organized schooling:

1. They don't want their kids to learn about sex on the playground from the kid whose dad subscribes to *Playboy*.

2. They'd die if Johnny came home using the f-word.

3. They think evolution is a federally sponsored lie.

4. The local private schools have become magnets for troubled rich kids.

5. They want to keep their kids from the Democratic Party members who use public schools as recruiting stations.

With dreams of a Falwellian utopia in mind, homeschool parents choose their child's academic regimen by buying or creating lessons with the support of thriving online homeschool communities. The best-selling homeschool curricula are:

McCarthy to Reagan: The Complete Hagiographies (FoxNews Press)

Christian Nation Rising: Official History of America, vol. 4 (Branch Davidian Books)

Kool Krafts for Kids (Duke & Co.)

HOMESCHOOLERS' LEAST FAVORITE FOUNDING FATHERS

If you have met a homeschooler, and actually had a successful social exchange, you probably appreciated his or her reverence for the Founding Fathers. Homeschoolers are quick to point out that the Founding Fathers were homeschooled, in those morally certain days when U.S. presidents owned slaves and dueling was a polite way to settle arguments.

But certain Founding Fathers run afoul of homeschoolers' approval:

THOMAS JEFFERSON: A vague deist who penned the noxious phrase "wall of separation between church and state" and knocked up a slave, which was worse than having a slave to begin with.

BENJAMIN FRANKLIN: Debauched womanizer—France suited him better.

ALEXANDER HAMILTON: A little tax-and-spend bastard.

JOHN MARSHALL: Pioneered judicial activism, paving the way for *Roe v. Wade*.

Inspired by the Amish, who have gained incredible social influence by withdrawing into theologically peculiar ghettos, homeschoolers hope to reassert America's Christian heritage and take back "their country" one great institution at a time, beginning with the National Spelling Bee. They believe that educational liberty sets America apart from the world's oppressive regimes, like the Taliban,

where homogenous groups of religion-minded children in tightly controlled environments learned only ideas approved by their religious leaders.

Here are some FAQs about homeschooling:

Do homeschoolers have recess?

Yes, in their backyards.

When do they take summer vacations?

Whenever they like.

Who serves as teacher?

Mom or Dad.

Who serves as principal?

Mom or Dad.

Who chooses the curriculum?

Mom or Dad.

What kind of special training do Mom and Dad need?

None.

HELPFUL HEADLINE

HARVARD FORCING HOMESCHOOLERS TO "FIT IN"

CAMBRIDGE, MASS.—Jim and Katrina Randalefner of Omaha, Neb., were shocked when, after driving all the way to Massachusetts to enroll their oldest son at Harvard

University, they discovered he'd been assigned to an all-homeschooler dormitory and forced to go through a program called "Fitting In" to help him socialize.

"It felt like segregation," says Jim.

But Harvard insists they're helping to mainstream students who otherwise find it difficult to blend in with the rest of the student body.

"The first year is tough for homeschoolers because many come from such limited social environments," says Kathy Kushner, coordinator of freshman counseling. "We wanted to help them get their footing."

Fitting In's semester-long schedule includes trips to parties where homeschoolers learn to have meaningless conversations to forge social bonds, tests on popular slang phrases, and lessons on how to "hang out" without outsmarting everyone else in the room.

But homeschoolers are offended by the assumption that they're socially stunted.

"This 'Fitting In' stuff is utterly risible," says Todd Randalefner, 17, looking up from the third volume of *The Rise and Fall of the Roman Empire.* "I consort with many types of people—Irish, Welsh, British, and many more. Just because I didn't have daily nutrition breaks or physical education in the traditional public school setting doesn't mean I need to be handled like some sort of fledgling titmouse. A titmouse is a small bird native to North America, three inches in length, and with a diet of insects and berries. Some species are endangered where urban construction has encroached on habitats."

Randalefner says he'll grit his teeth and stay in the dorms for one year. "Then I intend to opt out, posthaste, and get an apartment," he says. "I'd rather study during waking hours, and I can't tolerate too much interaction with people."

From LarkNews.com, a good source of Christian news

Chapter 10
EVANGELICAL
EDUCATION

SUNDAY SCHOOL

The second cradle of learning for evangelical children is Sunday school, where basic doctrines are taught with flannelboards and paper-cutout Bible characters, or, if the Sunday school teacher is feeling lazy, a VeggieTales video.

HELPFUL HEADLINE

SAVIOR SCOUT RELIEVED THAT PEERS CONSIDER HIM "NOT AS UNCOOL AS LAST YEAR"

GREEN BAY, WISC.—High school junior Dirk Smith, whose teenage years were devastated when peers learned he was still an active member of his church's Savior Scouts group, is delighted to learn that opinion leaders in his school consider him not as uncool as last year.

"He edged up in the polls, mostly because we heaped such abuse on him last year, we felt pity for him—for now," says one very cool kid who begged to be identified, but won't be because he's under eighteen.

Smith was humiliated when the newspaper ran a photograph of him in full Savior Scout uniform receiving an award from a regional commander. The Boy Scout–style uniform includes a neck scarf, an Air Force–style hat, slacks, a belt, and a short-sleeve shirt full of Christian-themed buttons.

Smith refused to be quoted, but local Savior Scout lieutenant Jeff Wilkes says he's distressed that anyone would tease him about being a Scout.

"God is proud of Dirk," says Wilkes. "And as an added bonus, Dirk will earn his Persecution badge for this."

From LarkNews.com, a good source of Christian news

Children are told to bring handfuls of coins for offerings, ensuring the church's financial future, and every Sunday they have the opportunity to meet Jesus, meaning that most evangelical children get saved hundreds of times before they reach adulthood.

In the middle grades, boys join the church's Boy Scout–equivalent group—called Savior Scouts, Royal Rangers, or the like—which combines outdoorsy activities with Bible study. Girls join Girl Scout–type groups with names like Daisies or Prims to learn the womanly arts.

By the time they reach middle school, evangelical children are intimately familiar with dozens of Bible stories, the most popular being:

David and Goliath

Noah and the Flood

Jesus and the disciples

Paul's missionary adventures

The least popular are:

David's adulterous affair (2 Samuel 11)

Noah gets drunk and passes out (Genesis 9:21)

Judas the disciple commits suicide (Matthew 27)

Paul shaves his head (Acts 18:18)

As they delve into Bible memorization, kids often compete in Bible quiz contests, which discourage familiarity with useless trivia about pop culture and encourage familiarity with useless trivia about the Bible. Bible verses become so ingrained in their minds that when evangelical siblings argue, it sounds like this:

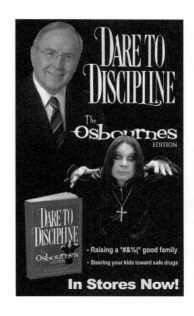

Chapter 10
EVANGELICAL EDUCATION

HELPFUL HEADLINE

AGING YOUTH PASTOR DRESSES, ACTS LIKE TEEN, YOUTHS SAY

ATLANTA, GA.—Forty-something-year-old youth pastor Bill Watson of Open Heart Church has embraced pop culture lingo and clothes in an attempt to ingratiate himself with the younger generation, say members of his youth group. He wears a goatee and ultra-baggy pants, drops the latest slang terms, and rides a skateboard around the church parking lot during his breaks.

"I thought he was twenty-two," says one teen. "Then I saw him at the grocery store with his sixteen-year-old daughter, and he's, like, a dad. It was creepy."

Watson refuses to confirm his exact age, saying, "You're only as old as you think you are."

"I'm just like the kids in my set," he insists after preaching a sermon freighted with pop culture references, which he reels off with practiced spontaneity. "We have a phat youth group, our activities are just sick. It's stupid the good times we have, dog."

But some kids look at him askance. Christina, 16, who's seen twelve youth pastors come and go during her three years at the church, said, "When I first saw him from a distance, I thought he was a high schooler. Then I got up close and saw he's balding underneath his baseball cap. I felt tricked."

Watson says he is working harder to fit in with his crew.

From LarkNews.com, a good source of Christian news

SISTER: Mom! Danny disobeyed Matthew 5:39 and bruised my arm!

BROTHER: I did not! She pulled a Genesis 31 with my toys, and so I did what David did in 1 Samuel 30:17.

MOM: I'm so angry that I feel like Jesus in Mark 3:5. You not only ignored Proverbs 10:23, but waltzed right over Luke 17 as if it didn't exist! Go to your rooms. I'll give you a taste of Hebrews 12 in just a minute.

SISTER AND BROTHER: Not that!

YOUTH GROUP

In junior high, evangelical teens join the church youth group, where they are expected to behave like model Christians in spite of their toxic levels of hormones. Youth pastors are tasked with the job of appearing as young and hip as possible while teaching teens the awesome pleasures of abstinence and keeping them from temptation with attractive alternatives like prayer meetings, street witnessing, and miming excursions to Mexico (aka youth mission trips). Some youth groups adopt names like eXtremely Radical 2:20, or Mission 4:18, which convey in cool lingo that being an evangelical is true rebellion against pop culture. The "2:20" and "4:18" Bible references imply exclusivity and secrecy, because when evangelical youths fancy themselves on a clandestine mission to convert members of a hostile culture, they make much better proselytizers.

There are four basic kinds of youth group:

Chapter 10
EVANGELICAL EDUCATION

LAID-BACK—Many groups hum along but don't amount to anything special. The kids learn the Bible and meet weekly for worship meetings, but the youth pastor has no particular ambition except to meet job requirements and enjoy his leisure time.

MILITARY ACADEMY—Some youth pastors want to train kids for end-times battles. Scripture memorization, intense sermons, and long prayer meetings are de rigueur.

MAKE-OUT DEN—Weak or absent leadership turns some groups into spin-the-bottle zones. The kids "pray" in another room while the youth volunteer reads a magazine and listens to praise music.

REVOLVING DOOR—Some churches cycle through youth pastors every six months because the position pays less than janitorial work or because the youth pastor can't keep his pants up.

Through youth groups, kids also attend church summer youth camps, which offer them their first chance to enjoy a spiritual retreat and see a bra run up a flagpole.

At a time of their choosing, evangelical children are encouraged to be baptized in water, following the example of Jesus. Water baptism is the closest thing evangelical culture has to a rite-of-passage ceremony and marks the day a youngster makes a public declaration of his or her allegiance to Christ. Churches baptize people virtually anywhere there

Through youth groups, kids also attend church youth camps in the summer, offering them their first chance to enjoy a spiritual retreat and see a bra run up a flagpole.

is standing water: in swimming pools, rivers, lakes, hot tubs, or the large tank or "baptistery" located in the sanctuary. Evangelicals prefer their baptisms the way some people like their doughnuts: dunked, not sprinkled. To evangelicals, flicking water at someone is an insult, not a baptism. Jesus was fully immersed (evangelicals say), and this method has the benefit of humbling you, as there is no vanity in looking like a drowned rat in front of the congregation.

CHRISTIAN COLLEGES

Evangelical education continues at Christian colleges, where clean-cut youngsters work feverishly to find a spouse and perhaps even earn a degree. The chaperoned approach to education appeals to evangelical parents, who are well aware that Yale and Princeton started as minister training institutions but now offer condoms in a dish by the door. Today's new breed of devotedly evangelical colleges offers a pleasantly conformist atmosphere where:

> **Professors pray before class**
>
> **Curfews and gender segregation are enforced**
>
> **Chapel attendance is compulsory**
>
> **John Ashcroft is often the commencement speaker**

For these reasons, Christian colleges and their sister schools, Mennonite technical institutes, have become the fastest-growing educational institutions in the United States behind online diploma mills, and all three offer degrees that are well respected in the temping industry.

Upon graduating, Christian college alums head confidently into the workforce, dazzling potential employers with their BAs in youth ministry and their experience leading the puppet team in San Salvador.

But to attract more applicants, many Christian colleges have recently refashioned themselves as "universities" and changed their names to hide their religious roots. This has created confusion in the marketplace, especially for non-evangelical applicants who are inadvertently drawn to the promise of "values-based learning in a small liberal arts environment," as brochures often advertise. To help prospective students distinguish between evangelical and secular colleges, here are the actual former names of today's leading Christian colleges:

Now Called	Used to Be Called
Anderson University (Anderson, Ind.)	Anderson Bible Training School
Azusa Pacific University (Azusa, Calif.)	Pacific Bible College
Belhaven College (Jackson, Miss.)	Belhaven College for Young Ladies
Biola University (La Mirada, Calif.)	Bible Institute of Los Angeles
Carson-Newman College (Jefferson City, Tenn.)	Mossy Creek Missionary Baptist Seminary
Chapman University (Orange, Calif.)	California Christian College
Eastern University (St. Davids, Pa.)	Eastern Baptist College

Christian college alums head confidently into the workforce, dazzling potential employers with their BAs in youth ministry and their experience leading the puppet team in San Salvador.

Now Called	Used to Be Called
Hardin-Simmons University (Abilene, Tex.)	Abilene Baptist College
Lipscomb University (Nashville, Tenn.)	Nashville Bible School
Malone College (Canton, Ohio)	Cleveland Bible College
Northwestern College (St. Paul, Minn.)	Northwestern Bible and Missionary School
Seattle Pacific University	Seattle Seminary
Taylor University (Upland, Ind.)	Fort Wayne Female College
Union University (Jackson, Tenn.)	Jackson Male Academy, and later, Southwestern Baptist University
Vanguard University (Costa Mesa, Calif.)	Southern California Bible College

Concerned mothers launch Obadiah Awareness Month

SAVANNAH, Ga. — Women from local churches have started a national campaign to raise awareness about the book of Obadiah, which they call the most ignored book in the Bible.

"People skip right over Obadiah to get to Jonah," said one woman tearfully. "I'm concerned about my children, and their children. What if they never read this precious book?"

The group penned a fight song whose melody is borrowed from the musical "Oklahoma." During the meeting they sang with gusto, "O-o-o-o-o-badiah, where Esau's house will not survive!"

ADULT EDUCATION

Throughout their adult lives, evangelicals keep up an educational regimen that puts even wealthy Connecticut book club members to shame. In addition to Christian education courses—Sunday school for grown-ups—men join "accountability groups," clusters of three to five men who meet weekly and pressure each other to love their wives and spurn pornography. In extreme cases, accountability groups become ganglike, with suburban white men hazing and harassing members who fail to show godly leadership in their families.

Women enjoy a full schedule of teas, women's luncheons, and retreats, most based on Proverbs 31, an obscure Old Testament passage that describes the ideal wife as, essentially, June Cleaver ("She gets up while it is still dark. . . . She sets about her work vigorously," and so on).

But the basic unit of social interaction is "small group meetings"—weekly home Bible studies that offer an intimate setting in which evangelicals grow to hate each other. Small groups gained popularity in the 1980s, when they were known as "cell groups" before terrorism took the phrase out of fashion. Devotional books provide the fodder for these Bible studies and for all individual study. Some devotionals sell millions of copies, to the consternation of the *New York Times Book Review*, which is forced to acknowledge them.

One of the most popular devotionals is *The Purpose-Driven Life*® by Rick Warren and the accompanying "40 Days of Purpose"® Christian training program created by Warren's® Saddleback Church® in Lake Forest, California. The program® leads participants through forty daily studies to help them discover God's will® for their lives. *The Purpose*®-*Driven Life*®, a sequel to Warren's® earlier bestseller, *The Purpose*®-*Driven*® *Church*®, examines the gospel® message at its most fundamental level, bringing participants® closer to Jesus® and to their life's purpose®. Warren's® website® puts it best: "The '40® Days® of Purpose®' campaign helps Christians® new and old find their purpose® in life®, for the glory® of God®."

MAN ENJOYS SMALLEST SMALL GROUP

WESTCHESTER, N.Y.—Stu Clark belongs to what is believed to be the smallest small group in America: himself.

"I meet at my house every week in the living room," he says. "I bring snacks and my Bible, and after some chitchat I get down to discussing that week's reading, sharing my burdens, my praise reports. Then I pray for myself."

He enjoys the intimacy he has gained with himself over the weeks, he says.

"There was a lot about me I didn't know," he says. "The small-group setting brings out those personal details you might not otherwise share."

He has tried larger small groups, but doesn't get as much from them.

"When you have to be social, it detracts from your real heart issues," he says. "Having other people in the picture complicates things. But I can deepen my relationship with myself much better if it's only me. There's a level of closeness you have when it's just one of you."

Stu's pastor has seen a marked difference in the man.

"He's definitely matured in his faith since starting the group," the pastor says. "I guess it's not the group size that matters, but the quality of the people in it."

From LarkNews.com, a good source of Christian news

Chapter 10
EVANGELICAL
EDUCATION

BEST-SELLING STUDY BIBLES OF 2005

Lactating Women's Study Bible (Nelson)

Double Your Income in 30 Days by Working from Home Study Bible (Tyndale)

Victoria's Secret Picture Bible (Knopf)

Some other best-selling devotional books are:

Growing Closer to God Than You Did Last Month (Zondervan)

You're Getting Warmer: More Incremental Steps Toward Intimacy with God (Thomas Nelson)

Now You're REALLY Close: The 2005 "Almost There" Devotional (Multnomah)

The Radical Teen's Funky-Awesome Life Path Adventure Devotional, with commentary by television superstar Kirk Cameron! (InterVarsity)

The Big Jabez Book of Crossword Puzzles (Multnomah)

VARIETIES OF EVANGELICAL POLITICS, FROM RIGHT-WING TO WACKO

No evangelical education is complete without a heavy complement of conservative politics. Evangelicals decided

Jimmy Carter was the first "born-again" president, but disappointed evangelicals by confessing his sins to a "skin" magazine (rather than to Rosalyn or to his accountability group) and quaffing Billy Beer.

in about 1976 that Jesus's earthly ministry was essentially political and that he had intended to take over the Roman government precinct by precinct, using "get out the vote" drives and putting voter guides in synagogues each November. He was thwarted by a run-in with Roman authorities that turned out badly, but 2,000 years later evangelicals wish to fulfill Christ's goal by gaining control of the modern secular superpower and bending it toward their idea of morality.

Jimmy Carter was the first "born-again" president, but disappointed evangelicals by confessing his sins to a "skin" magazine (rather than to Rosalyn or to his accountability group) and quaffing Billy Beer. So the evangelical community threw its support behind an army of divorced Republicans—Ronald Reagan, John McCain, Dick Armey, Phil Gramm, John Engler, Bob Dole, Pete Wilson, John Kasich, Susan Molinari, and Newt Gingrich—who at least understood that the Bible allows for divorce if your staff assistant is cuter (see Matthew 5:31). As a group, these politicians came to represent America's Moral Majority.

PROVERBS 31 WOMEN

Laura Bush
Kathie Lee Gifford

NOT PROVERBS 31 WOMEN

Pamela Anderson
Gloria Steinem
Barbra Streisand
Ellen DeGeneres
The cast of *Sex and the City*

GAY NIV BROADENS BIBLE'S APPEAL

GRAND RAPIDS, MICH.—Zondervan, the publisher of the New International Version (NIV) translation of the Bible, is publishing a revised version dubbed the gNIV, aimed at a homosexual audience. The editors made subtle changes throughout the text to "provide more entry points for gay readers," says Brad Ebbelstein, Zondervan director of marketing.

"There's a lot of ambiguity in the original text, so we felt at liberty to make different assumptions based on the perspective of homosexual readers," says Ebbelstein.

For example, he says, in the standard NIV the passage about a rich young man who asks Jesus how to gain eternal life reads, "Jesus looked at him and loved him." In the gNIV, this is changed to, "Jesus looked at him and was supremely attracted to him."

The Study Version also asserts that some of David's Psalms were written to his homosexual lover, Jonathan. In side notes King Saul is depicted as a father who couldn't accept his son's sexual preference.

"It's about bringing this inspired book up to date and making it culturally relevant to a segment of the population that, frankly, feels condemned by most other Bible translations," says Ebbelstein.

Gay leaders applauded the new translation.

"We applaud Zondervan for taking our perspective into account when translating the Good Book," says Maurice Fritzson of Gay People for Fair Treatment. "You might say this version is NIV-positive."

From LarkNews.com, a good source of Christian news

Here is how evangelicals interpret Bible passages to arrive at their political positions:

This passage . . .	really means . . .
"Remember the poor" (Galatians 2:10)	Remember how lazy the poor are and thank God you're not on welfare like them.
"My kingdom is not of this world" (Jesus in John 18:36)	But for now, make sure you keep control of the White House and Congress.
"Give to Caesar what is Caesar's, and to God what is God's" (Jesus in Matthew 22:21)	Only pay taxes on money you can't hide from the IRS.
"Thou shalt not kill" (God in Exodus 20:13)	Kill only those who deserve it—like death row inmates, abortion doctors, sworn enemies of the United States, and the French, when possible.
"Do not mistreat an alien or oppress him" (God in Exodus 22:21)	Vote against government benefits for illegals.
"The Lord God placed the man in the Garden of Eden to tend and care for it" (Genesis 2:15)	Don't worry about the environment because when Jesus comes back he'll destroy the earth anyway.

SOUTHERN BAPTISTS, REPUBLICAN PARTY MERGE

WASHINGTON, D.C.—The Southern Baptist Convention and the Republican National Convention have decided to merge, citing similar constituencies.

"There's so much overlap, it just makes sense," says Marc Racicot, chair of the RNC.

The merger—the largest by any religious or political body in U.S. history—gives birth to the newly named Southern Baptist Republican National Convention, or SBRNC, a major new force in politics and doctrine.

"In general, we Baptists will cover Kingdom stuff, and the Republicans will handle Caesar's side of things, but there'll certainly be cross-over," says transition supervisor Bruce Danzinger.

From LarkNews.com, a good source of Christian news

In spite of their political success, evangelicals still believe their values are under siege. Issues like gay marriage, abortion, gay marriage, prayer in schools, gay marriage, and especially the homosexual agenda haunt the evangelical mind. Without the calming tones of Bill O'Reilly and (thrice-divorced) Rush Limbaugh, evangelicals might lose heart, and all their education would be for naught.

Chapter 11

PARTYING LIKE AN EVANGELICAL

I t's time to celebrate! You have successfully surveyed evangelical culture from top to bottom. You know how evangelicals greet each other, their decorating habits, where and why they attend college, even how they make love. To cap off your accomplishment, throw an evangelical party! Use the knowledge you've gained in this guide to create a magical night for your evangelical friends. If you have no evangelical friends, you can gather a crowd by hanging flyers in local churches that look like this:

Food, fellowship &

FREE DESSERT

(Your address)
(Time and date)

AMBROSIA

1 can chunky fruit cocktail, drained
1 can mandarin oranges, drained
1 can pineapple chunks, undrained
1 cup whipping cream
1 cup miniature marshmallows
$\frac{1}{2}$ cup shredded coconut
$\frac{1}{2}$ cup chopped walnuts

Combine fruit ingredients, stirring to blend. Fold in whipping cream, marshmallows, coconut, and walnuts. Refrigerate until serving time. Serves one.

THEMES AND SEASONAL PARTIES

When inviting people, you should describe your party as a "time of fellowship," a "get-together," or a "potluck." Avoid words like "kegger" or "blowout," which bring to mind post-Lent Catholic festivities, or "soiree," which smacks of Paris salons. The party should not involve morally questionable themes like swimming, hot tubs, pajamas, togas, wine and cheese tasting, or charity fundraising. Indeed, free food is all the theme you need.

Holiday parties are acceptable, but stay clear of holidays like Cinco de Mayo and St. Patrick's Day, which evangelicals believe are merely excuses for drinking. For Christmas parties, skip Santa Claus decorations and deck the house instead with crèches and angels. For Easter, stay away from the Easter bunny, an intolerable interloper to most evangelicals on their most sacred day.

CHURCH PICNIC RUINED WHEN COUPLE BREAKS LIL' SMOKIES PLEDGE

TACOMA, WASH.—Two hundred people who had anticipated Living Way Church's annual picnic were gravely disappointed when the couple who signed up to bring a Crock-Pot full of Li'l Smokies bathed in barbecue sauce forgot the dish.

One by one, attendees at Gann Park scanned the rows of food.

"Where's the Smokies?" one man asked his wife. She whispered that they had been forgotten. In anger, the man cracked his plate in half and threw it in the trash, then repaired to a nearby tree to smolder.

The Moore family, who had volunteered to bring the Li'l Smokies, sat with grim expressions. Nobody approached them, save one reporter.

"We blew it," Doug Moore said. "We signed up for it, and then forgot."

A few feet away, people had left a spot on the table by the card that read, "Moores: Li'l Smokies," hoping that the picnic favorite might miraculously appear. Some stared at the spot in silence.

"We remembered the A&W root beer," Sandy Moore said, trying to inject a note of grace.

Meanwhile, an atmosphere of gallows humor prevailed. The pastor shook people's hands and made nonspecific comments like, "We'll do better next year. It's okay." The volleyball net sat idle. Nobody donned the gunny sacks for the usually festive 100-yard dash.

Timothy and his wife Rhonda sat on the grass holding plates of cold, uneaten quiche, mayonnaise-heavy macaroni salad, and pretzels. Their children played tag around the monkey bars.

Chapter 11
PARTYING LIKE
AN EVANGELICAL

"I told the kids I'd get a game of softball going, but I don't feel like it," Timothy said. "There's a hole in my stomach where those Smokies should be."

Frustrated organizer Jim Braswell found it hard to settle down. "They put their signatures on the sign-up sheet," he said. A few others were considering formal action against the Moores, he said, perhaps stripping them of small-group host home status or compelling them to chaperone the junior high kids at church camp. But most people didn't want punishment, just a taste of their beloved barbecue-flavored dish.

After a while the Moores slipped away quietly, taking their untouched A&W two-liter bottles. Then the rest of the group dispersed.

From LarkNews.com, a good source of Christian news

Halloween parties are strictly off limits, but you may substitute a Harvest Festival and put hay bales, cornstalks, and other symbols of fecundity at the door. Have guests bob for apples, fish for prizes, and toss Ping Pong balls into goldfish bowls to win WWJD bracelets. Naturally, your guests will not wear witch, ghoul, or vampire costumes.

If you have a New Year's Eve party, make it a "watch-night" meeting where everyone prays for the year to come. Serve sparkling apple juice, celebrate the new year at 9:00 P.M., and send everybody home.

PREPARATIONS

Once you've decided what kind of party you will have, hand out invitations in several church foyers after Sunday services. Then try to snag a marquee guest who will add sizzle to your gathering—a pastor, evangelist, or, best of all, a missionary fresh from the field. This person will give your event spiritual significance. During the meal you can quiet everybody and have the missionary share his latest yarn from Africa, or have the pastor make heartwarming remarks, or have the evangelist give an altar call.

Ready your house for the big night by removing shot-glass collections, beer lights, "Women of . . ." calendars, objectionable CDs and DVDs, ashtrays, corkscrews, wine-glasses, brandy snifters, humidors, cigar cutters, Native American art and dream-catchers, lingerie catalogs, maga-zines of left-wing commentary, lottery tickets, poker chips, casino chip buckets, photos of the family in Vegas, modern art, and any Far Eastern furniture, unless you are prepared to say you bought it on a short-term mission trip. Trans-form the liquor cabinet into a display of Bible quiz trophies (have some made for the occasion), and put a well-worn devotional book in the bathroom magazine rack. If neces-sary, rent a storage unit to hold your non-evangelical knickknacks. You don't want nosy kids stumbling on your bourbon collection or other unmentionables. See chapter 8 for a decorating refresher.

It's unthinkably rude to ask evangelical parents to leave their children at home, so set aside an entire room for youngsters to watch a video. Buy a Noah's Ark playset and a set of Twelve Disciples plush toys for the smaller ones, and consider hiring teenage evangelical girls as babysitters. If it counts as credit toward their homeschool home economics unit, they may do it "as unto the Lord," which means for free. Prepare another room for nursing mothers—it will be well used. Place chairs in corners throughout the house to give homeschoolers a comforting place to read their latest biographies of John Adams.

Chapter 11
PARTYING LIKE AN EVANGELICAL

Set the tables potluck-style with paper plates and Styrofoam cups, which lend a cozy feel, redolent of church basements and fellowship halls. Evangelicals don't have dietary restrictions—not on your life—but your menu should include nothing more exotic than what you find in the Costco freezer section. A basic menu will look like this:

Li'l Smokies bathed in barbecue sauce, served in a hot Crock-Pot

A big bowl of ambrosia (see recipe)

Potato salad, heavy on mayo

Enchilada casserole

Jell-O with tangerine wedges

Brownies

Don't bother with veggie platters, which will only make guests feel guilty. Do *not* serve liqueur-flavored desserts, like rum cake or amaretto mousse parfait. Even a strong presence of vanilla can turn evangelicals against you. Avoid this culinary gaffe—eschew distilled ingredients of any kind.

SETTING THE MOOD

Before guests arrive, cultivate an atmosphere of openness and purity. No dim lighting, which makes evangelicals feel like they've wandered into a lounge. Choose music beforehand, sticking with popular worship albums of the day. You might get away with playing U2, the world's leading undeclared evangelical band, or Bob Dylan's

Evangelicals don't have dietary restrictions—not on your life—but your menu should include nothing more exotic than what you find in the Costco freezer section.

Christian albums (circa 1980), or even Charlie Daniels or Randy Travis, country artists who crossed into the Christian market after their careers tanked. But to stay on safe ground, brave the Bible bookstore and purchase several upbeat praise albums, preferably by bands from Great Britain or Australia, to show your hip Christian sensibility. But avoid Amy Grant, who might seem an obvious choice. She disillusioned fans when she left Christian music, divorced her Christian husband, and married a country singer of dubious spiritual commitment. Hearing her music might put your guests in a funk.

When people start arriving, hug them at the door and tell them the Li'l Smokies are warming up. Invite them into the well-lit living room and usher their children to the kids' room. As hungry as they might be, evangelicals will never start eating until someone has blessed the meal with "a word of prayer." This duty should fall to the pastor or person of highest clerical rank, even if it's the nursery coordinator. Without an opening moment of prayer, the party would take on a worldly cast.

TOP CHRISTIAN RAP RECORDS

(Talkin' 'Bout) My Wife's Booty (Christ Kreww)

Prazen' Till I'm Dazen' (JC Maxx)

Devil's Dis'n Ya'll (Salty)

Do Da Ho-ly Thang (Jive Temple)

My God Is Phat (Tha Gospel Digz)

As you mingle, encourage an atmosphere of joy but not wildness, familiarity but not flirtatiousness. There shouldn't be too much cross-gender conversation, for the sake of propriety. You shouldn't have to prime too many conversations, because there are no chattier people than evangelicals enjoying free eats. But be ready anyway with conversation starters like, "Why don't you tell us how you met the Lord, Joe?" Or, "Debbie, how'd the clown performances go in Venezuela?" Avoid lines you might normally use, like, "Bob, this is Denise. She's unhappily married too," or, "Talk among yourselves. I'll go see how the margarita mix is holding up."

If you wish to jazz things up with a game, lean toward something silly, not risqué. Avoid games that involve teaming up with someone else's spouse or passing objects from person to person without the use of hands. Trivial Pursuit is out, unless you have the Bible version. Rook, the evangelical version of poker, is acceptable, as are Bible charades and mixers centered on questions like, "If I could be any Bible character except Jesus, I would be. . . ."

Remember to step back and enjoy what's happening. Your study of evangelicals has brought you to this unique moment. While you may have started out frightened or ignorant of them, now your home is full of evangelicals, laughing, back-slapping, and standing in line for their fourth serving of pigs in a blanket. Your guest bedroom is being destroyed by evangelical children bored with the VeggieTales video they've already watched two hundred times since it came out. People are becoming pleasantly sedated and lapsing into the couch with dreamy thoughts of heaven and another scoop of ambrosia. Real live evan-

Remember to step back and enjoy what's happening. Your home is full of evangelicals, laughing, back-slapping, and standing in line for their fourth serving of pigs in a blanket.

gelicals are talking about answered prayers, personal devotions, and how they received a touch from God at the last evangelistic crusade. You might even hear them exclaim, "Glory!" when they get excited. This is your moment! Revel in it.

PARTY PITFALLS

But in all the fun, be on guard against potential problems. At secular parties, the host must occasionally deal with rowdy guests, boors, and drunks hitting on the married women. At evangelical parties, the host must watch instead for guests whose gaucherie or spiritual fervor can derail the good feeling. Beware of the following.

Amateur Prophets, Faith Healers, and Exorcists

Pentecostal/charismatic guests who have slipped into the mix may try to practice their "spiritual gift" on others, adding a note of discomfort to the esprit de corps. Some charismatic individuals fancy themselves prophets and believe God gives them messages he wants delivered to people. These people start conversation with the words, "God gave me a word for you." The "word" usually involves a deep-seated hurt you are supposedly hiding and concludes with a promise that you will have an international ministry once you yield this hurt to God. These people can make other guests uneasy and provoke doctrinal fights.

    Other evangelicals believe they have the gift of healing. They cruise the room listening for any mention of illness

Some evangelical women will see your gathering as a golden opportunity to market the dishware, jewelry, or candles they sell through their home-based businesses.

or disease, then interrupt to say, "God has given me the gift of healing. Do you mind if I pray for your kidney problem/fibromyalgia/illness brought on by overeating?" They will want to lay hands on the person, which could create a spectacle, especially if the "healer" patterns his style after Benny Hinn.

Still other evangelicals believe they have the gift of discerning spirits, meaning they can tell when someone is unwittingly possessed by a demon. Spotting a "demonized" person, they often move swiftly to cast it out, grabbing the person's head and shouting loudly enough to establish their spiritual authority and to ensure that the demon hears them.

If any of these sudden outbursts brings your party to an awkward halt, politely draw the zealous person aside and ask him to "save it for the sanctuary." If he turns on you and declares you are "quenching the Spirit," then you have no good option. In your most guttural, hellish voice, offer the prayer warrior some enchilada casserole or Bundt cake. It may not solve the situation, but your Baptist guests will get a kick out of it, and the joke should lighten the atmosphere.

One important exception to this rule: Often during conversation an evangelical will express a "need" that prompts others to lay hands on him or her in spontaneous prayer. This is perfectly acceptable, and evangelicals with any cultivation are trained to handle these impromptu ministry moments discreetly and without display. This may happen dozens of times without you knowing it, and it will add spiritual heft to your party because it shows guests that the Holy Spirit is at work.

Also beware of:

Women with Home-Based Businesses

Some evangelical women will see your gathering as a golden opportunity to market the dishware, jewelry, or candles they sell through their home-based businesses. If your party is a potluck, at least one woman will show up with an extravagant, multilevel serving platform designed to pique other guests' interest in her entire line of useful kitchenware. She may place a catalog on the potluck table and stand by to answer questions.

Though it's terribly déclassé, eager women may even distribute invitations to their upcoming candle or kitchenware parties. The only way to dissociate yourself from them is to hang a sign near the potluck table that reads, THIS FELLOWSHIP EVENT IS NOT AFFILIATED WITH ANY HOME-BASED BUSINESS OR MULTILEVEL MARKETING SCHEME. PLEASE REPORT ANY HOME-BASED BUSINESS ACTIVITIES TO THE HOME-OWNER.

Guests Who Won't Leave

Single people will want to stay as long as possible, hoping to discover their soulmate somewhere in your living room. Unless you are vigilant, your home could host an all-night rap session for singles bemoaning that God hasn't given them a spouse yet. Wrap up some of the leftover food, if there is any, and put it in their hands to hurry them along.

CONCLUDING YOUR PARTY

The party should last two hours and not go past 9:30 P.M. Nothing wholesome happens after dark, unless you and

your spouse have just discovered the LaHayes' sex book or you're at an all-night prayer meeting. Adjourn by asking a guest to close in prayer. It's customary to select someone on the spot by saying, "Let's have a moment of prayer. Dan, will you do the honors?" Dan will step forward and give a quick prayer, unless Dan is the associate pastor, in which case he will give a short sermon to scratch his leadership itch. After a rush for the table to polish off any nubs of remaining food, your guests will gather their children and head for the door.

You may, if you wish, give party favors purchased at the Bible bookstore—combs, key chains, and refrigerator magnets gold-stamped with Bible verses. These would be a welcome surprise. At the door, squeeze people's necks and say, "See you later, should the Lord tarry." This will send them away with warm thoughts of the Rapture.

The best part about evangelical parties is that, while you may feel bloated the next morning, you won't wake up hungover or with someone in your bed who looked a lot better in dim lighting.

Congratulations! You are now fully equipped to identify and interact with evangelicals wherever you encounter them. Keep this field guide handy—and enjoy!

The Legend of the Sand Dollar

There's a pretty little legend
That I would like to tell
Of the birth and death of Jesus
Found in this lowly shell.
If you examine closely
You'll see that you find here
Four nail holes and a fifth one
Made by a Roman's spear.
On one side the Easter lily
Its center is the star
That appeared unto the
    shepherds
And led them from afar.
The Christmas poinsettia
Etched on the other side
Reminds us of His birthday
Our happy Christmas time.
Now break the center open
And here you will release
The five white doves awaiting
To spread goodwill and peace.
This simple little symbol
Christ left for you and me
To help us spread his gospel
Through all Eternity.

        —AUTHOR UNKNOWN

Footsteps in the Sand

One night a man had a dream.
He dreamed he was walking along
the beach with the Lord.

Across the dark sky flashed scenes from his life.
For each scene, he noticed
two sets of footprints in the sand,
one belonging to him and the other to the Lord.

When the last scene of his life flashed before him,
he looked back at the footprints in the sand.
He noticed that many times along the path of his life
there was only one set of footprints.
He also noticed that it happened at the
very lowest and saddest times in his life.
This bothered him, and he questioned the
    Lord about it.

"Lord, you said that once I decided to follow you,
you'd walk with me all the way.
But I have noticed that during the most
troublesome times in my life there is
only one set of footprints.
I don't understand why when I needed you most
you would leave me."

The Lord replied: "My precious, precious child,
I love you and would never leave you.
During your times of trial and suffering,
when you see only one set of footprints in the sand,
it was then that I carried you."

—AUTHOR UNKNOWN

GLOSSARY OF EVANGELICAL TERMS

ALTAR CALL The summoning of sinners and the unsaved to repent, often at the altar area near the front platform.

ANOINT WITH OIL To dab the forehead of a prayer recipient with oil, symbolic of the touch of the Holy Spirit.

"AS UNTO THE LORD" Describes work done for free.

BABE IN CHRIST New convert. Also YOUNG IN THE LORD.

BACKSLIDE Willfully depart from a moral lifestyle and/or Christian commitment.

BIBLEMAN A fictional evangelical superhero created and acted by former *Eight Is Enough* superstar Willie Aames.

"BOW YOUR HEARTS" A way of asking people to bow their heads and close their eyes for prayer.

BROTHER IN THE LORD/SISTER IN THE LORD Fellow born-again Christian.

BURDEN A feeling of concern for a person or situation, interpreted by evangelicals as requiring their prayer or action.

CHICK, JACK Best-selling author of often-chilling Christian tracts.

CHURCH FAMILY One's fellow church members.

CHURCH WORK DAY Day when people volunteer to perform various tasks relating to the upkeep of the church facility.

DEVIL'S DRINK Alcohol.

DEVOTIONS Regular time spent in Bible reading, prayer, and meditation. Also **DEVOTIONAL**, any inspirational or meditative book written to facilitate devotions.

DIVINE APPOINTMENT An unplanned meeting that seems to have been orchestrated by God.

EVANGEL-ASTIC A humorous term meaning "overstated," deriving from evangelists' tendency to exaggerate.

EVANGELISTIC CRUSADE Series of meetings designed to "save" lost people.

FAITH PLEDGE A promise to give money one doesn't have, and doesn't know how to procure, usually to a building program.

FEEL CONVICTED To feel guilty for one's sinful behavior.

FELLOWSHIP Socialize.

FELLOWSHIP HALL Large room in a church for social gatherings and potlucks.

FIRE INSURANCE Derogatory term for salvation when a convert's only motive is to escape hell.

FLOCK Congregation.

FROZEN CHOSEN A humorous term Christians use to describe apathetic congregations.

GOD THING A circumstance or idea that God is perceived to be guiding or causing (slang).

HALLELUJAH OR ALLELUIA Hebrew word meaning "Praise ye the Lord."

HARVEST A large number of conversions.

HEALING LINE Line of people waiting to receive prayer for healing at a healing service.

HYMNAL A songbook of time-tested praise songs.

"I LOVE YOU IN THE LORD" An appropriate way of expressing friendly affection.

INTERCESSION Prayer on behalf of others.

LOVE OFFERING A free-will offering, usually collected for guest evangelists in lieu of set payment.

OFFERTORY The song played while the offering is collected.

GLOSSARY

OUTREACH Evangelistic effort.

PAUL The apostle Paul, author of much of the New Testament.

PLANT A SEED To instill the gospel message in someone's mind without necessarily leading them to Christ.

PRAISE REPORT Announcement of answered prayer or good news.

PRAYER CHAIN A loose but potentially numerous affiliation of people committed to pray for prayer requests, often relayed by telephone or Internet.

PRAYER CIRCLE A local group of intimately connected people committed to praying for one another.

PRAYER MEETING A gathering of Christians to pray. Can be held anywhere, from a living room to the church sanctuary.

PRAYER REQUEST A petition for others to pray to God on behalf of a specific need.

THE RAPTURE The event when Christ snatches born-again Christians away from Earth and into the air. *Note:* The term "Rapture" does not appear in the Bible.

REBUKE THE DEVIL To speak against the devil in hopes of driving him out of a circumstance or person.

THE REDEEMED Born-again people.

REVIVAL Similar to an evangelistic crusade, but focused on reviving the saints to higher levels of enthusiasm for the gospel.

RING THE BELL Preach a good sermon.

SACRIFICE OF PRAISE The sincere effort made to praise God by humbling oneself, often with singing and lifting one's hands.

SECOND COMING The second coming of Christ to earth, when he will establish himself as ruling king.

SEEKER-FRIENDLY CHURCH (ALSO SEEKER SENSITIVE) A church that downplays religious rituals, symbols, and lingo to attract non-Christians.

SHEPHERD Pastor. Also **GOOD SHEPHERD** for Jesus.

"SHOULD THE LORD TARRY" Phrase used to remind other evangelicals that all plans are subject to the sudden occurrence of the Second Coming.

SINNER'S PRAYER Prayed on conversion, recognizing one's sinfulness.

SLAIN IN THE SPIRIT To faint and fall to the ground, overcome by the Holy Spirit, usually after prayer from a visiting evangelist.

SPIRITUAL WARFARE Confrontational prayer against perceived demonic forces.

SMALL GROUP A regularly occurring, home-based Bible study meeting of people who attend the same church.

SWORD The Bible. Also THE WORD.

TESTIMONY The story of how one came to Christ.

TITHE One-tenth of one's income.

GLOSSARY

TOUCH FROM GOD A special feeling of God's response to a particular need; in some circles implies an actual miracle.

TRACT Small evangelistic brochure, often illustrated with eye-catching cartoons.

"UNDER THE BLOOD" Describes a sin that has been forgiven and forgotten.

UNSPOKEN REQUEST Prayer request given without stating the specific need.

VEGGIETALES The best-selling Christian computer-animated children's video series of all time.

WAIT ON GOD A quiet, anticipatory posture toward God regarding a certain situation.

WARREN, RICK Best-selling author of *The Purpose-Driven Life* and pastor of Saddleback Church in Lake Forest, California.

WITNESS A verb meaning to share one's testimony of Christ.